FLYFISHING
THE HIGH COUNTRY

John Gierach

PRUETT **P** PUBLISHING COMPANY

First Edition

5 6 7 8 9

Library of Congress Cataloging in Publication Data

Gierach, John, 1946-
  Flyfishing the high country.

  1. Fly fishing. 2. Trout fishing. 3. Grayling fishing. I. Title. II. Title: Fly fishing the high country.
SH456.G57   1984   799.1'755   84-4805
ISBN 0-87108-662-X (pbk.)

Printed in the United States of America

FLYFISHING THE HIGH COUNTRY

Table of Contents

Acknowledgements

THE AUTHOR WISHES TO thank Keith Bilby for his invaluable technical assistance in the preparation of this book. Special thanks are also due to A.K. Best, Koke Winter, Mike Clark, Dave Student, Bill Purdy, Carole VanOstrand, Clark Everest, Gil Lipp, Ed Engle, Jim Pedley, and Paul Hinchcliff for help, advice, encouragement, aggravation, argument, confusion, wader patches, and the occasional free meal.

Photography Credits:

Front cover, John Gierach; back cover, photograph of the author, Christy Ross; page 22, Carol Haytas; all other photographs by John Gierach.

Introduction

ALL FLY FISHERMEN HAVE their practical, even scientific, side, but deep down most of us are romantic and nostalgic. We tend to want things to stay the way they've always been, and I think it's that part of the sport that draws us into the high country. Conditions in the mountains can be fickle and changeable, but there's also a permanence that is both fascinating and comforting.

The mountains—any mountains—can make you pay for your fishing with time, shoe leather, exertion, and even disappointment. But they usually give back more than they take in terms of solitude and a sense of adventure that you just won't find on more civilized waters.

High country waters cannot, of course, be lumped together under a single heading. Some are overpopulated with brook trout and produce only small fish, some are rich in food organisms, and many others are sparse. You may find cutthroats, brook trout, goldens, rainbows, grayling, or an interesting mix of two or more species. Sometimes they'll be maddeningly difficult to catch, and sometimes they'll be idiotically easy—and those two extremes can be encountered on a single piece of water in just one day.

In many cases, a healthy high country lake, stream, or beaver pond will yield fish no larger than ten or twelve inches—sometimes not even that big—but in many cases the big fish are there. Sometimes that's because the habitat is unusually rich, and sometimes it's in spite of the fact that it's very harsh.

How big is big? In my experience, fish in the fourteen-or fifteen-inch class are excellent in most high country waters, but they do get bigger. My friend Keith Bilby, a crack alpine lake fisherman whose brains I've picked often over the years, has taken brook trout, cutthroats, and goldens in the five- and six-pound class from high mountain lakes. If trout like that don't excite you, please write to me in care of the publisher and tell me where you fish.

I'll hasten to point out that trout like that are exceptional, and catching them is almost always the result of considerable skill and knowledge and more than a little hard work. Still, such fish are up there, and they *can* be caught. That fact alone can make a range of mountains look even more beautiful than it already is.

This book will not give you detailed directions to specific waters and, though the selfish reasons for that are obvious, they're not the only ones. Some of the spots I know of were found through my own hard work and research, but others were the result of tips given to me by other hard-working fishermen. And if the sport has one cardinal rule, it's that one shall not break a confidence.

Also, many alpine fisheries are very delicate and just can't stand up to much fishing pressure. I've seen more than one spot get fished out in a single, short season once the word got out, and once a spot is ruined, it comes back slowly, if at all.

In fact, at least one major American fishing magazine asks potential contributors not to "hot spot" waters that might be harmed by the increased pressure an article might generate. Bravo. Of course, few of us can find it in our hearts to keep a great spot entirely to ourselves, but keep in mind that everyone you tell will probably tell someone else and so on.

Finally, although I've fished the high country for quite a few years now and try to discover one or two new spots every season, I still know of only a handful of good high country trout waters in the mountain west. This book is designed to show you how to locate the best waters for yourself, in whatever mountain country you're fishing, and, once they're found, how to fish them to the best advantage.

As I look over this manuscript, I see that I've included a lot of words like "sometimes," "often," and "usually" and statements like "when conditions permit." That's because nothing is "always" true, especially when you're talking about high country trout fishing, and because every lake, pond, and stream on every particular day presents a unique problem. Dumb luck aside, I think the solutions to fishing problems are best found in a solid understanding of the situation at hand, not in step-by-step directions in a fishing book.

The tactics, techniques, and fly patterns discussed here have all worked, but they should be considered as a good starting point rather than as the final word on the subject. A willingness to experiment and to deal with unusual or even weird conditions is the mark of a good fly fisherman. The best fishermen I know try not to make the same mistakes over and over again; instead, they always strive to make new and interesting mistakes and to remember what they learned from them.

Working the weedy shoreline of a high lake.

The High Lakes

I SHUDDER TO THINK OF ALL THE big trout I've spooked out of the shallows of alpine lakes by just charging up to the bank or into the water, eager to fish and elated at having the heavy pack off my back and the long walk over. I can close my eyes and picture their long, dark shapes darting for deep water, never to be seen again.

I've gotten better about that in recent years, but I still do it, especially on lakes that I think I know well. Now, when I top the last ridge or round the last bend in the trail, I tell myself, "Okay, just relax and watch."

Wading in and starting to fish too soon is the most common mistake fishermen make on high country lakes, or any other trout water for that matter. There are, naturally, times when you'll want to slog out up to your armpits and work the deep water, but that usually is the last thing you should try, not the first.

Let's say you've just arrived at an alpine or high country lake. It doesn't matter if you've fished it many times before or if this is the first time—step one is to deposit the pack well back from the bank and, from a good distance, survey the water.

It's difficult to describe the typical high country lake because they are all unique. But for the purposes of illustration, let's say this one is fairly small (no more than a few acres), has a rocky bottom, a relatively shallow shelf running at least part of the way around the lake, and a deeper hole more or less in the middle. It may also have a stream inlet and an outlet where the stream gathers itself together and continues downhill. There may or may not be large, exposed rocks, weed beds, deadfall trees, and other structures.

The surface of the lake may be peppered with rises—always a welcome and beautiful sight—but let's say you can't tell just by looking at it where the fish are or even if any are there at all.

The first thing to do is scout the shallow water near the bank. I like to patrol the shoreline for a while, staying as far back as possible while still being able to see into the water, trying to spot cruising fish.

The shallow water of a high lake (what's known as the littoral zone) is where most of the aquatic insects live and where most of the windblown terrestrial bugs are deposited. Therefore, it is logically the most likely place for fish to be feeding. You'll sometimes see single fish (the biggest ones are often solitary), but many high lake fish tend to cruise around in loose schools, making them easier to spot. Cutthroats, rainbows, and grayling are the most likely to school, brookies almost never.

How much of an area a pod of cruising fish will cover depends on any number of variables, not the least of which I like to think of as their current mood, but if insects are concentrated in a certain area (a hatch of caddis flies, a weed bed full of freshwater shrimp, or a fall of flying ants, for instance), the most active fish will probably stay in a single bay or inlet.

Sometimes they'll work erratically, milling around on a shelf for a while and then disappearing into deep water, only to turn up again in a few minutes, sometimes in the same place, sometimes in another. On rare occasions, I've seen loose schools of fish cruise all the way around a lake, taking as long as an hour and a half to make the circuit of a ten-acre body of water. I haven't seen this often enough to make a real judgment, but my guess is that it happens when very little food is in or on the water.

This tactic of spotting fish in the shallows presupposes two things: clear, still water and a good pair of polarized sunglasses to cut the glare. The way some polarized glasses are marketed these days makes them look like gadgets, but they're not—they're among the most valuable pieces of gear a lake fisherman can own. If the light is wrong or the wind has put a chop on the water, you can still spot fish, but it's a lot more difficult.

Rises, boils, and wakes on the surface will betray the presence of fish, but unless there are a lot of insects on top, cruising fish tend to rise only sporadically to the odd bug. You may also find that it's the smaller fish who rise freely to the surface while cruising in search of food, while the larger ones stay deep, looking for easier prey. Rises are always an encouraging sign, but don't get carried away and go right to the dry fly. That's an excellent way to catch a lot of small fish and no big ones.

Also keep in mind that trout are well camouflaged when seen from above, and just because you don't spot them, even under ideal conditions, doesn't mean that they aren't there. One of those big trout that I remember spooking came from a shallow bay that I'd studied carefully for a good twenty minutes and then waded into after having decided there were no fish close to shore. The fish was about an eighteen-inch brookie, and he'd been there the whole time. He was holding in about a foot and a half of water, and I almost stepped on him. I also never saw him again. Apparently, he'd just been sitting there, and that was the main problem. When you spot a trout, you see a little movement rather than a whole fish. Once you've seen the first one, others will often materialize in the same area.

The point here is, always work the shallow water first, no matter how sterile it looks or how tempting the dark water over the dropoff looks. If conditions permit, that is, if you're not up against a stand of trees or a rock cliff, start casting from a position well back from the bank and work your way out. If you were right and no fish were there, you'll only waste ten or fifteen minutes. If you were wrong, you may be greeted by the wonderful sight of a trout materializing out of the shadows on the bottom, heading for your fly. That only needs to happen a time or two before the lesson is learned.

Of course, the first cast may spook fish that you didn't see, and you'll be greeted with the not-so-wonderful sight of trout fleeing in terror. That's when the wise fisherman laughs at himself and learns the lesson anyway.

Trout in shallow water are naturally spooky, and great caution is required when casting to them under these conditions. A trout is chased by all kinds of predators from the day he hatches (even before, for that matter), and even when he's grown to a size where his only enemies are ospreys and man, he retains that legendary shyness that has made him such a classy game fish. These fish seem especially attuned to attack from above, and that's how your fly line landing on the water will be perceived. Sometimes just the shadow of your line will do it. Think of it this way: a trout follows a single rule when there's any undue disturbance on the surface of shallow water—"hide."

Fly tackle has improved considerably since 1676, when Charles Cotton advised anglers to "fish fine and far off," but no one has ever improved on that statement. When working the shallows of a high country lake, stay as far from the fish as your casting ability allows, and fish a long, fine leader. Under the most difficult conditions (very spooky fish in very clear, still water), the ideal situation would be for the fisherman to be well back from the bank throwing a cast where the line lands on the ground and only the leader strikes the water.

If what's behind you on shore doesn't allow for this, you might want to get into the water a little way down the bank and cast parallel to shore, but make sure that you're not wading into a pod of fish in *that* spot. In other words, where you're casting *from* can be just as important as where you're casting *to*.

That's an extreme case, but if you fish the high lakes often enough, you'll sooner or later come on just such a situation. The other extreme—one you'll also probably come upon sooner or later—is where the fish don't seem to care about you, your fly line, or anything else, and you'll be getting strikes almost at your feet. This kind of situation is most likely to happen with brook trout (little ones at that), sometimes with cutthroats, rainbows, or grayling, and seldom (one might even say never) with goldens. Nine times out of ten, you'll find yourself somewhere in between.

In the still, shallow waters of a high country lake, I'll usually fish a leader that's no shorter than nine or ten feet with a tippet no heavier than 5x. Sometimes I'll go as light as 7x, although a friend has suggested that you don't need to go that light. He may be right. The difference in diameter between 5x and 7x leader is only about two thousandths of an inch, while the difference in breaking strength is significant—somewhere between one and two pounds of test. It's a good argument, but I've been in too many spots where stepping down leader size seemed to be the key to success, so I still do it. I also seem to do better if I use smaller flies in these situations unless I'm trying to match a specific bug that I think the fish are feeding on.

As I mentioned before, if there's a chop on the water your chances of spotting fish are greatly decreased, but there's also an advantage to this situation: a little bit of a riffle will cover your cast better and allow you to get away with being a little closer and using a heavier tippet and larger fly.

Fishing writers have long been fond of attributing specific personality traits to the different species of trout, but, although there is definitely some merit to this approach, I believe the environment plays a very large part in determining how a trout will act. Many high country lakes are rather sparsely populated with food organisms when compared with, say, a Pennsylvania spring creek, and the growing season is typically short. This means that a fish has to be an aggressive and opportunistic feeder to be successful.

It's true that golden trout, as a rule, tend to be the shyest of the high country fish, that brookies and grayling tend to be the most aggressive and the most open to suggestion (the most likely to race four feet to grab a Royal Coachman, for instance), and that the cutts and rainbows will usually fall somewhere in between. Still, I think it's fair to say that all of these fish, when they're found in the high mountain lakes, tend to be opportunistic rather than selective feeders.

This is why so many of the good high lake fishermen I know do the majority of their business with nondescript wet fly or nymph patterns of the Hares Ear or Zug Bug variety. Most of the high lake fish can be fooled into grabbing a #12 Hares Ear Soft Hackle, even if they happen to be feeding on something entirely different at the time, because it looks alive and, thus, good to eat.

The wet fly has the further advantage of being down at the fish's level (assuming it's fished at the proper depth) so the fish doesn't have to expend a lot of energy to take it. The decision to rise to the surface seems to be a hard one for a trout to make unless there's a lot of insect activity on top of the water.

Still water nymph and wet fly tactics can vary greatly, and that's another advantage they have over dries. You can fish at a variety of depths and with various speeds and styles of retrieve, some combination of which will often do the trick.

When working the shallows for cruising fish, the best results tend to come if you can drop the fly well ahead of the fish, let it sink down to slightly below the level at which the trout is moving, then start a slow retrieve right in front of the trout's nose. Even if he's never seen anything like it before (and if it's a Zug Bug, there's a good chance of that), he may well take it out of curiosity and because it's just too easy. The take can be impressively casual.

Naturally, the ideal conditions required for this tactic to work (excellent visibility, fish that don't veer off at the last minute, and so on) don't always come together on a regular

A good fish on, in a small high lake.

basis, but some variation of this tactic is usually the most consistent way to take cruising fish in shallow water.

Since trout and grayling often cruise around the shallows in apparently random patterns, you'll often find yourself having to drop the fly only a foot or so in front of them, and this is where I prefer a smaller fly that makes less of a splash when it hits the water. At times the fish don't seem to mind a fly plopping onto the surface—sometimes they'll even be attracted by it—but it's usually fair to assume they won't like it very much, and you should try to cast as far ahead as possible.

When the visibility is poor, you're reduced to using the same tactic blind. You won't know if you're casting to a spot where there are no fish at the moment or are dropping the fly right on top of them. Happily, the conditions that will most often limit visibility in shallow water—a breeze, a cloudy day, or a light spatter of rain—will tend to make the fish a bit less spooky. It sounds like it might even out but, in my book at least, it doesn't. I'll take clouds and wind over excellent visibility anytime.

The speed and style of your retrieve will have as much to do with your success as any other factor, including pattern. The answer may be a slow, crawling hand twist retrieve, a fast swimming strip, or something in between. As a general rule, trout that are cruising lazily seem to be more interested in the slow crawl, while those that are darting around chasing bugs want a faster strip. The fly should act more or less like the trout because the trout are probably acting like the real bugs. When in doubt, start off slowly and gently—you'll be less likely to spook the fish.

If no fish are working the shallows, try at any stream inlet or outlet—anywhere there's a current. The inlet of a healthy stream will usually be pumping in a small but steady supply of aquatic bugs, and it's always possible there will be a full-blown hatch going on, in which case the insects will be concentrated on the area of the lake right at the inlet. If the bugs are just filtering in a few at a time, you may find only small fish working the inlet, but if there are good numbers of bugs, then the larger fish may well move in. Also, a little hatch that doesn't amount to much on the stream can really turn into something when the bugs start to collect at the lake inlet.

A good strong outlet can serve almost the same purpose, collecting the floating insects from the surface of the lake and delivering them, in a gentle current, to the waiting fish.

I got into an interesting situation like that a few years ago on a cutthroat lake. The only place fish were working was at the outlet, and only in a little twenty-by-thirty-foot piece of water where the current really started to pick up. The water was glass-smooth until the last second, when it went over a little shoulder-high falls into the creek. My partner and I couldn't see a thing on the water, not even a speck, but the trout—maybe twenty fish altogether—were rising steadily. We could see the fish pretty clearly in the smooth water, and they were darting around some, not just holding in one spot. We took that to mean they were very interested in what was on the surface but there weren't a lot of bugs, whatever they were. The fact that we could see absolutely nothing on the surface from a good vantage point under almost perfect conditions meant the bugs were either flush floating (like a mayfly spinner) or very small (like midges) or both.

It was a one-man spot, so we flipped a coin and my friend took his turn. He also took a fish on the third cast with a #18 black deer hair beetle. I don't carry that pattern, so when my turn came I tried a #18 spinner and took a fish.

Between us we took a dozen fish from that spot (resting it for a few minutes now and then), and we were successful with five different patterns. I don't think that's too unusual, and I've seen it a number of times. It's rare to find a concentration of a single kind of insect at an outlet. I almost always use a small, low-floating fly in a situation like that with the smooth, clear water and all, but someday I'll get up the nerve to try a #10 Royal Humpy, just to see if it works.

If it's spawning time, the fish may be concentrated at the inlets, the outlets, or both. It's hard to resist trying to hook one or two fish at a time like this, if only to have a look at their bright, spawning colors. But for obvious reasons, it's best to leave spawning fish alone or, at the very least, to release any you may catch.

Another good place to try is around any structures that provide cover. Even when trout aren't feeding, they will often hang out around jumbles of rock, sunken brush, weed beds, and the like, and they generally won't be too lazy to grab the odd nymph that happens by. Trout may also be cruising lazily in the neighborhood of structures, giving the angler the advantage of having his fish confined to a relatively small area. Always keep an eye on offshore structures for the quiet, solitary riser.

But let's assume you've scouted the shallows, worked the stream inlets and outlets, and cast to the offshore structures with no success. An hour or two has gone by and it's possible that things have changed—things *do* change on high lakes, often and quickly—but chances are you're finally ready to work the deep water over the dropoff shelf.

You're looking for fish that are either cruising the deeper water or who are just suspended, waiting for the proper weather, time of day, a bug hatch, or whatever it is that trout wait for at such times. In any case, the best tactic is to wade out until you can reach the deep water with an easy cast and start searching with a weighted nymph. It's best to start relatively shallow and work deeper, using a slow retrieve first and then a faster one. The sharpest dropoffs are often the best, but the gentle slopes can be good too. If there are different kinds of habitat, work one for a reasonable amount of time—until you're satisfied that if fish are there, they've seen your fly—then try the other. If there's a weed bed on an otherwise rocky bottom, try that first. A steep dropoff near a stream inlet is also a good shot.

So far, we've been fishing with a floating line and a weighted nymph on a long leader. For deeper water you can add a split shot or two to your leader for greater depth, but a rig like that is horrible to try and cast any distance. Better yet, go to a sink-tip line. A sink-tip will go down faster than

Working the deep water in a mountain lake.

even a weighted nymph, so it's best to use a short leader to keep the fly as deep as the line—maybe even as short as two feet.

I like a fairly large nymph for this kind of work, a size 10 or 12, and I try not to change patterns or sizes until I've given the fly I'm using every chance to produce. I'm convinced that in most high lake situations it's not the specific fly pattern that makes the difference, but where and how it's fished.

This kind of fishing is slow, even tedious, if you're not in the mood for it, but it can sometimes yield big fish (though seldom on a regular basis). If you decide to take a pass on this take a nap or a lunch break and wait for something more exciting to happen, I'll forgive you.

Now, having made a case for fishing nondescript wet flies over nonselective trout in the high lakes, I'll devote some space to the exceptions. There are *always* exceptions in trout fishing—that's why we stay interested.

Selectivity usually happens when a lot of one kind of insect is available and, though this is the exception on most high country lakes, it's far from unheard of. What insects and other food forms you find in a mountain lake will depend on dozens of factors including water chemistry, bottom composition, elevation, mean summer water temperatures, vegetation, and so on. Midges are common, as are mayflies, caddis flies, and freshwater shrimp (scuds), and you may even find damsel and dragonflies, aquatic beetles, water fleas, and leeches.

I know of a lake (a small pond, really) in Colorado's Roosevelt National Forest that gives up good hatches of various species of midges, mayflies, and caddis which are backed up by large numbers of dragonfly and damselfly nymphs and aquatic beetles. It seems more like a bass pond than a trout lake—it's that rich—but it's above 10,000 feet. The trout are typically opportunistic when the insect activity is slow, but during heavy hatches and spinner falls (which are common through midsummer and into the fall), they can become maddeningly selective. The brook trout, as you'd expect, are quite large. I think I know of a five-pounder that came out of that lake, but the man who caught it has never really admitted that was the place. Fair enough.

When you come on selectively rising fish in a high lake, regardless of the hatch or the pattern you're using, you'll be faced with the same problem you had with visible cruisers in shallow water: you have to put the fly where the fish is going to be, not where he just was. Leading fish can be difficult when you can see them, but when you're dealing only with rise forms, it can be downright frustrating. However, if you spot the rise of a big fish you think is worth singling out from the crowd, give a little time to figuring out what his pattern is, then lead him with your cast and an educated guess. If all else fails, cast two feet to one side or the other of a good rise and hope he's going in that direction.

If you're like me, you'll guess wrong better than 50 percent of the time.

A number of very competent high lake anglers will tell you that streamers don't work in these waters because the trout aren't likely to eat other fish and because there are no forage fish anyway. But I've caught too many high lake fish on streamers to leave them out of this discussion. Most were brookies, some were rainbows, and a few were even cutthroats. In fact, fishing a streamer is sometimes a good way to eliminate the little fish and hook some of the big ones.

Last summer I was on a small lake, the smaller of two, up in the Indian Peaks Wilderness Area. It was a perfect cutthroat day—overcast, cold, with a fitful breeze—and trout were rising all over the lake. My two partners and I were connecting well, using a variety of smallish wet flies, but all we were getting were little cutthroats, from seven inches on down. I knew there were good fish in the lake and the weather was ideal, so I kept working that wet fly and getting little trout.

Finally I waded out near the dropoff, replaced my wet fly with about a #8 Squirrel Tail Streamer, and started working the edge of the dark water. After only a few casts I felt a good strike, the kind where you can really feel the weight of the fish. He started into a strong, steady run, and all of a sudden the weight got very heavy and very dead: a rock.

Since I'd lost my fly anyway, I went ahead and put on a heavier leader and another streamer, and within the next half hour I landed a sixteen-inch brookie and a fifteen-inch cutt. Those were the only good fish I landed that afternoon, but they were enough to make the day a success, and I'm convinced I'd never have hooked them except on the streamer.

I typically try a streamer in one of two situations: when I'm taking fish with such regularity that I feel confident to experiment or try to single out the larger ones, or when I'm doing so badly that desperation has set in. They have often worked at both times.

Streamers seem to be most effective out near the dropoff

or in deep water, and medium to small flies—sizes 6 or 8, sometimes as small as a #12—seem best. I fish them pretty much the same way I fish wet flies and nymphs except that I usually start with a little faster retrieve.

The weather in the high country can change at a moment's notice, and these changes exert a strong influence on insect and fish behavior. Everyone, myself included, likes to be up in the mountains on a bright, warm, sunny day, and the fish will certainly feed at these times. I've found, however (and many good fishermen concur), that the best days are overcast and cool, and a breeze or even a drizzling rain or snowfall can make for excellent conditions. As a friend of mine puts it, "hypothermia and cutthroats go together." I don't keep a detailed fishing log, but I'd guess that I've taken a good 80 percent of my larger high lake fish under conditions that, in another context, I'd call "bad weather." I believe this is because the low light and the cover of a ruffled surface make the fish, especially the larger ones, more confident about exposing themselves. You will, naturally, have to find your own happy medium between getting soaked and frozen—something that can be dangerous, even fatal when you're far out in the backcountry—and fishing at what is often the best time.

Wind can be both a blessing and a curse on a mountain lake. A stiff breeze can make casting a chore, and long casts can be almost impossible if you're facing into the wind. At the same time, a wind can ruffle the water nicely, trap hatching insects on the surface, and even deposit terrestrials that wouldn't be there otherwise.

Trout and grayling will sometimes decline to feed right on the surface when it's windy, probably because the bugs are hard to see on the choppy surface. But they will often begin to rise well when, and if, the wind dies down. In some cases, especially when cutts are involved, they'll keep rising to a choppy surface, but you just won't be able to see them.

Like fishing in a drizzle, fishing on a windy day will require you to put yourself in the most uncomfortable position. If the wind is blowing out of the northwest, then the leeward side of the lake (the northwest side) is where the casting is easiest. Unfortunately, most of the insects and fish will collect on the windward side (the southeast in this case), and that's where you should be fishing—right into the wind.

The high mountain lakes are best described as unpredictable and paradoxical. You can come on a high lake at mid-morning and find no indication whatever that there's a single bug or fish in it and then, an hour later, be fishing to hundreds of trout rising to a multiple hatch of midges, caddis, and mayflies. You may fish a lake four times and come to believe that it holds nothing but six-inch cutts and then, on the fifth trip, hook a five-pound brookie, or, just as likely, spook him in the shallows because you've gotten too casual, thinking you know all there is to know about the place. You'll never know it all, and that's where the fascination comes from.

Working the tail of a small high country beaver pond.

The Beaver Ponds

UNLESS YOU'RE THINKING in terms of geologic time, the lakes and rivers are permanent—barring some natural or manmade disaster, they'll always be there. No so with beaver ponds. A pair of beavers wander up a small mountain creek. They build a dam that creates a pond, go about their business, and maybe their descendants move on up to build other dams. In time, though, either the dam will blow out in the spring runoff and the pond will revert back to a stream, or it will silt in to become dry land again and be covered first with willows, later with aspen and pine. It's a slow process, but it happens quickly enough so that you can see it going on.

There's a pond near my home that I used to fish ten years ago. It is all but gone now (silted in), and the ten-inch brookies I used to catch there have been replaced by the same four-and five-inchers that were in the creek before the beavers came. I also remember fondly another one that was shared by some big cutthroats and grayling that vanished suddenly one spring when the old dam, probably battered down by an ice jam, just gave way. I haven't gone up there to look at it—don't think I want to see it—but a friend told me you could see the tracks and other signs in the mud showing where raccoons feasted on the fish. It's sort of like the difference between growing old slowly and gracefully and getting killed in a car wreck.

On the other hand, I know of a few ponds that never seem to change, or that change too slowly to be noticed by the fisherman who goes back year after year. I'm sure there are good and logical reasons why one pond will silt in in a dozen years and another will stay the same for decades, although those reasons are not obvious to me—probably the same kind of complex blend of events that makes big trout in one place and little ones in another. Whatever the case, a good beaver pond is a wonderful and unique place.

Some flyfishers like to think of beaver ponds as miniature lakes. That's a useful, if not always accurate, comparison, but if you're going to make it, you have to extend the analogy to cover the whole situation. If a beaver pond is a tiny lake, then you are an enormous fisherman. The shadow of your rod is like a tree waving over the water, and your footsteps, telegraphing across the spongy ground of the meadow, sound like boulders falling. In other words, stealth is the key.

Although I've seen a few really large beaver ponds—ones that covered as much as two or three acres—the typical mountain pond tends to be fairly small and shallow, no more than a few feet deep at the dam and through the old stream channel. It's easy to spot fish in water like this, and, especially with a new pond that you don't know anything about, it's very tempting to just walk over to the edge and see if any trout are in it.

The problem here is that you'll see some fish, but they'll also see you, and the only ones that won't spook will be the little dumb ones that you're not interested in. Trout in a beaver pond are like the trout in the shallows of a lake: they seem to know they're exposed and they tend to be skittish. Of course, the middle of the pond has no deep water to run to like in a lake, but there will be cut banks, logs, the dam itself, and other cover, and it's surprising how effectively a big trout can disappear in a little pond.

A lot of fishermen will make the "little brookie" assumption about a beaver pond. They'll walk right up to the nearest bank—maybe perch up on the dam or even wade in a little—and proceed to take four or five little fish. "See," they'll say, "little brookies."

In some cases they'll be right, but in a surprising number of others they'll simply have executed a self-fulfilling prophecy—they'll have spooked whatever big fish were there, caught a few of the young, aggressive ones, and moved on. That's not just a literary device. I have, in fact, seen a lot of people do that on ponds I knew to hold better fish, and I can write about it with confidence because I've done it often enough myself (and recently, too, not just when I was a kid and didn't know any better.)

In my own defense, I'll say that most of those times were when I'd stumbled on some ponds on the way to a lake and didn't plan to fish them unless I spooked some good fish, in which case I'd come back in a day or so. Once I had the chance to glass some ponds from about a hundred yards (and at some elevation), and that was just about perfect. I could see every inch of water without disturbing things in the slightest. I don't carry binoculars, but I happened to be out for a walk with a bird-watcher that day.

Maybe I shouldn't have used brook trout as an example of small fish here, because brookies are the most likely specie to overpopulate a pond and produce all those little fish. All things being equal, a pond with any other specie or mix of species (cutthroats, rainbows, goldens, grayling) is more likely to have good-sized fish.

But even brook trout can grow large in a beaver pond on a cyclical basis. The typical scenario goes something like this: a pair of beavers builds a dam on a creek with some small brook trout in it. The pond appears in a few weeks and constitutes a sudden and significant improvement in the habitat. Almost overnight there's deeper water, flooded brush, more underwater surface area for insect habitat, deep water and cover at the dam, and so on. It becomes a classic, textbook trout pool instead of a ragged little stream.

The few little trout that find themselves there with their fortunes vastly improved begin to grow at a rate faster than normal for the creek. There won't be a lot of competition because there won't be a lot of fish, and so naturally the fish will get big. They'll continue to breed—that's what brook trout do best, and they can accomplish it almost anywhere—and before too many years have passed a bunch of little fish will be present in the pond again. But until that first generation of fish dies off from old age, there will also be some big trout, maybe even the kind you measure in pounds instead of inches.

It's been speculated by some that the bigger brookies will feed on the little ones, thus greatly increasing their growth rates, but others—fisheries biologists among them—will tell you that brook trout don't eat little fish, even when they're hungry and are closed up in the relatively small space of a pond with a whole bunch of fish. All I have to say about that controversy is that big brookies—and little ones, too, for that matter—will take streamers and that many of our classic streamer patterns were developed around the brook trout fisheries of the East. We think of streamers as little fish imitations, but there's no telling what the brook trout think of them. In fact, it's probably closer to the truth to say that they don't think at all, they just react.

This state of affairs—little fish that are easy to see and catch and big ones that aren't—can exist with any kind of trout or with grayling and, if the pond isn't fished properly, it's easy to take a few of those little fish and write the whole place off. And (I'll say it again) fishing a beaver pond properly involves stealth.

The most likely place for a trout to be rising in a pond is where the stream enters and a little current is present. A place like that will act like the head of a pool in a trout stream in that the fish can lie in the more comfortable slower current and have the insects brought to them, getting lots of calories while expending very little energy.

In a lot of ponds you can almost figure on a couple of fish always being up at the head somewhere, either in the current tongue or alongside it, taking whatever odd mayfly or drowned beetle the stream has to offer. There may also be a couple down at the tail of the pool, just in front of the dam, where the current picks up again. If a good, heavy hatch is going on, these are prime spots and may well be taken by the best fish in the pond, but when insect activity is sporadic, as it often is, the fish you see in these spots will probably be small ones. We fly fishermen are suckers for rising fish, and it's always tempting to try them, but in a pond that you know—or think—holds better fish, it's worth taking a quiet look around.

Many beaver ponds have flooded brush and trees, logical and obvious holding areas. Brush and trees in the water provide shade, cover, and surface area for aquatic insects and, unless the fish are actively rising or cruising, they'll almost always choose to hang out around structures of some kind. Pay special attention to these areas.

A good fish in a pond may be doing any number of things. If he's rising, you're in business. Assuming you can spot him by his rise form or the boil he makes on the surface, you only have to get into position for a cast—not always as easy as it sounds, of course. During a heavy hatch, the big fish will likely take up the best feeding station, but really heavy hatches are rare, and the fish is just as likely to be off the current or even back in an eddy somewhere. Keep in mind that the first few obvious risers probably aren't the only ones coming to the top to feed. In a pond with a fair amount of surface feeding going on, look for the solitary riser.

Catching the bigger fish on dry flies is a fine experience, but those trout seem reluctant to come to the surface on a regular basis unless there's some very good reason. In fact, I think you stand a better chance of pulling a good fish to the surface in a pond by slapping a big Humpy up against the bank than by casting imitations of those little Red Quills that keep petering down the stream.

The big fish rising in a beaver pond is most likely to be the cruiser who's working the banks and the flooded brush, taking most of his food under the surface and rising occasionally for the beetle or caddis fly that he happens to spot. Next to a steady hatch, this is the best situation in which you can catch a fish. He's actively feeding and looking for food, which means that he's not keyed on a specific bug and is open to suggestion. In a beaver pond, he's also in a fairly small space where you can keep track of him. Sometimes in a lake you'll see a trout the size of a small torpedo swim by and never see him again. In a pond, you can usually locate him again if you're careful and patient.

As in a lake, a big, solitary fish will sometimes seem to cruise randomly, and sometimes he'll exhibit a pattern. It's not unusual for a fish to want to work a certain kind of spot. In a beaver pond, that might mean the face of the dam, a stretch of flooded timber, or a current backwash at the head. Now and then you'll find a fish cruising back and forth along a ten-yard stretch of bank like a duck in a shooting gallery and you can lead him easily. More often he'll be wandering around, but he's still likely to stay in a given area.

I'll usually try to get a fish like this on a weighted nymph or wet fly in about a size 14—something that's big enough for him to trouble himself for but not so big that he's never seen anything like it before. If I can see him, then I naturally try to lead him, casting the fly in front of him, letting it sink, then starting a slow retrieve just as he comes on it.

If I can't actually see the fish regularly and am only catching glimpses of the occasional rise, I'll wait for that glimpse or rise and cast near it but not right on top of it.

I'll sometimes go for a fish like this with a dry fly, and it's a little like bass fishing. You toss a #14 Adams, or something like it, near where you think the fish is and just let it sit there in the surface film, giving it an occasional gentle twitch. My personal rule here is that if the rises are gentle and slow— what you might call lazy—I'll figure the fish isn't all that taken with whatever is on the surface, and I'll go with the wet fly. If the rises are splashy and vigorous, even if there aren't a lot of them, I'll figure he really likes the dry fly and I fish the Adams. If I *really* want the fish, either because he's that big or because I haven't been doing well, I'll go to the wet fly. Most times it's the better bet.

So far we've assumed ideal conditions: the fish are rising,

the water is calm so that you can spot the cruisers, and you've managed to stay low and quiet and get into position to make your casts without spooking every fish in the pond. That's a lot to ask, but it's amazing how careful you can get when working over good trout. I know people who can't even park a car but who can move through willow thickets like a wisp of smoke when there's a fourteen-inch cutthroat to cast to.

If it's an overcast day or the evening or morning light is low and slanting, it won't be as easy to spot fish, but they'll also probably feel a little safer at these times, which is to your advantage. A breeze that riffles the water makes it next to impossible to spot fish, but it also covers your cast and approach and is among the best of conditions. The best you can hope for—the best beaver pond day—is cloudy with a cool, riffling breeze.

In a situation like this you'll be fishing water instead of working to individual fish, and the best way to start here is from the dam side. A beaver dam is a natural trout blind—you can come up on the pond from the downstream side and poke only your head and your casting arm over the top. In most cases, the stream behind you will provide room for a hassle-free backcast, something that beaver pond flyfishers spend a lot of time praying for.

You'll want to fish a wet fly when you're searching so the little current at the back of the pond can be incorporated into your retrieve. You can cover a lot of water from behind the dam, and by the time you have to stand or climb up for distance, you'll be working a long enough line that it won't matter.

I think trout move around a lot under choppy water (though I'm not sure why), so I try to be very methodical. I cast as many times as it takes to cover the water in front of the dam in a fan pattern about twice (more if I'm getting strikes), then lengthen the cast a few feet and make another fan and so on. It's hard to spot boils and rises on choppy water, and there probably won't *be* a lot of rises. But if I think I see something, even if it's just out of the corner of my eye, I'll always cast to it. For a long time, when I'd catch some little flash or curl in the current—something I wasn't sure I'd even seen at all—I'd think, "Probably nothing." At some point along the line I started casting to them anyway, and I have been pleasantly surprised enough times that now I think, "Probably *something*." It's downright startling to realize the things that occur on the surface of the water that we don't allow to register in our minds.

There *is* one thing wrong with fishing a pond from the dam side: your line will get caught in the sticks in the beaver dam. Notice I didn't say "may get caught" or "might get caught." Your line will sooner or later get caught, even if you hold it in loops in your line hand. And when you're caught in a beaver dam, you're looking at a minimum of five minutes to get loose, only to have it happen again a few minutes later. I think the beavers do something to the sticks to make them attract fly line.

Just six weeks ago I had a good brookie on in a beaver pond, and I was fishing from the dam. I was fooling around with light tackle that day because it was clear and bright, so I had him on a 6x tippet and a #20 dry fly. The fish, which turned out to be right at fourteen inches, wanted to run, and the line, of course, was hopelessly braided into the dam. I had to play him like you'd play a catfish on a stick and a string, but I landed him anyway, giving me a new respect for 6x monofilament.

So why hide behind the dam? Because beaver pond trout are spooky and you've got to stay hidden, even at the cost of tangled line. However you approach a beaver pond, from whatever direction, it's important to keep low or stay behind something. It's also important to walk softly because the ground in most beaver meadows is soft and spongy and will telegraph a heavy step for many yards.

Each situation is different, but beaver ponds, with their brushy willow banks, can be a nightmare for a fly caster. Still, if at all possible, use a sidearm cast, at least when you're working in close. It doesn't make much sense to go to a lot of trouble to stay hidden and then wave an eight-foot stick in the air. The fact that the best place to *cast* from is not always the best place to *fish* from probably goes without saying.

A beaver pond is an interesting tactical problem, because in any small, exposed water situation, one or two fish landed—or even a few clumsy casts—can easily spook the whole place, and the big fish will spook first. This means that the biggest fish you'll take from a beaver pond will usually be the first one, and *that* requires some thought and planning for the first approach.

Beaver pond fish are seldom selective to pattern because, like most high country waters, heavy and concentrated hatches are not typically common. Most days a few general patterns will suffice if you fish them well. There are, however, exceptions.

The pond I'm thinking of is one of the biggest I've ever seen—bigger than a lot of alpine lakes. The stream comes down a steep canyon into a small hanging meadow, where it branches. Beavers have dammed both branches, flooding the entire meadow and making a fine lake with two deep channels and lots of flooded spruce trees. I've often wondered if that just happened or if the beavers planned it that way.

The stream itself is almost totally uninteresting. It's small, fast, and shallow with only a few little pools holding a few little fish. The pond, however, holds some of the largest beaver pond cutthroats and grayling I've ever seen.

A friend and I camped at this pond for two days a few years ago. During the day, we took some eight- to ten-inch grayling from the loose, cruising schools and the odd cutthroat of about the same size from the flooded timber. Not bad at all, but bigger fish were there and they showed themselves in the evenings when a midge hatch came off.

The midges hatched from a deep, muddy-bottomed corner of the pond, and the fish that rose to them were noticeably larger than the ones we'd taken and seen during the day. Normally we'd have seen at least some of those hefty fish during the day's fishing, but this was a very big pond with some deep water.

To shorten the story a little, the fish turned out to be

maddeningly selective. We stepped down our fly and leader sizes until we were fishing #24 midge pupas on 7x tippets, and that was when I hooked the big cutthroat. I never saw it myself, but it went right past my friend on its way into the flooded timber across the pond. He told me later that it would have gone "at least twenty inches." I tried to turn the fish, but it was a useless effort on that light tackle. He took me into the trees, tied me off neatly, and broke the leader. Twenty inches? Well, maybe, maybe not. Like I said, I didn't actually see it.

That would have been the largest beaver pond trout of my career. I might have stood a chance with a bigger hook and heavier tippet, but he was just too selective to be fooled by anything like that.

Although I *have* seen good hatches of midges, mayflies, and caddis on beaver ponds, insect emergences tend to be sporadic, like in the high lakes, and the fish will remain open to suggestion most of the time. Most beaver ponds don't generate a lot of aquatic vegetation, so freshwater shrimp are rare, but "lesser" trout foods like leeches and water beetles may be present. In ponds (and lakes, too) that hold those fast-swimming beetles known as backswimmers or water boatmen, a small, fat, wet fly fished with a quick, jerky retrieve can be deadly.

In ponds that lie out in an open meadow, as many do, the fish have to rely chiefly on aquatic insects, but terrestrial bugs (ants, beetles, and, at the lower elevations, grasshoppers) may form a large part of the trouts' diet in ponds that are surrounded by trees or brush. These are good places to locate those big, solitary bank feeders.

Operating on the usually correct assumption that the fish aren't selective, I'll usually attack a beaver pond with something like a #12 or #14 Hares Ear Soft Hackle or Zug Bug. A big trout rising back in the flooded timber might require a dry fly like an Adams or an Elk Hair Caddis, though hatches or spinner falls will sometimes (though far from always) require you to more or less match the size and action of a particular bug.

Especially in ponds holding brookies or rainbows, a small streamer will sometimes produce. My favorite beaver pond streamer is a little thing known locally as a Gray Squirrel Tail. I tie them in the smaller sizes, say, 8 through 12, and try to fish them fairly deep. Sometimes I'll go to this fly after I've taken a few fish on or near the surface, and at other times I'll start with it, especially on a big, deep, juicy-looking pond.

The best time to fish a beaver pond, like a lake, is under low light (mornings, evenings, and cloudy days) or when there's a little chop on the water. The worst time is in the middle of a clear, calm, bright day. On a pond that you know to hold large fish, the wisest thing might be to wait out better conditions, fool around camp, take a nap, or fish up stream for a mile, then come back when things look more promising. It's even more important to hit a pond right than it is a lake, because the smaller scale and conditions that help you keep from advertising your presence are your greatest advantage.

A nice looking piece of water on a high stream.

The High Streams

I COULD SAY THAT FISHING the high mountain streams is pretty much like fishing trout streams anywhere except that most of them are smaller and claim a world record for the shortest chapter ever in a fishing book—but I won't. Although that's largely true, there *are* a few fine points worth talking about.

The high country streams (or creeks or brooks or whatever you want to call them) are the headwaters of the larger streams lower down and, if you want to get technical about it, of the big navigable rivers and the oceans. When you follow any mountain-born drainage upstream, the creeks branch and branch again like the roots of a tree, getting smaller and colder all the time. A few of them end at lakes and remain fishable for the greater part of their lengths, while many just dissolve into unfishable trickles.

The St. Vrain River, the stream that runs in front of my house, is a textbook example. Down here it's considered to be a fifth-order stream—the result of five major tributaries—but that's deceptive because dozens of tiny feeders flow into it here and there, most of which are both nameless and fishless, and some of which don't even run the whole year.

In the main branch and a ways up both major forks, you'll find lots of brown trout and some rainbows, but then, at a point that seems to move around from year to year, you'll start running into brook trout and maybe even the odd cutthroat. For lack of a better definition, this is when I consider myself to be in the "high country." It also *looks* like the high country up there, with high, rocky crags, steep canyon walls, and pine and spruce along the banks of the streams instead of willow and cottonwood.

The majority of this area is pocket water, but there are some good pools and flats scattered along if you know where to find them, and the fishing is often, though not always, better in those spots. Higher up are some beaver meadows with ponds and, higher still, the feeders from the high lakes and snowfields come in.

By the time you're high enough to really be into brook trout, the stream has split into three major forks, and somewhere on those three you can find any type of classic trout water that you can imagine, though you'll sometimes have to hike miles of pockets to get there.

There are some long, slick glides and bend pools that remind me of the Henry's Fork of the Snake in Idaho (on a smaller scale, of course), and there are braided fast-water runs that look just like parts of the Madison in Montana. On the North Fork is a series of stair-step plunge pools that could have been lifted right out of the South Platte River in Cheesman Canyon in Colorado. Don't ignore these similarities when you come upon them. Trout are trout, and water is water, and the fish will likely be in the same places doing the same things.

This is just one stream system—the one with which I'm most familiar—but the point is that any mountain stream can be, and usually is, full of surprises. This is a typical healthy mountain stream drainage in that there are trout in just about all the water that's fishable, and their size and numbers are determined by the kind of habitat in which they find themselves. Some of it is quite good, and much of it, depending on your definition, isn't worth fooling with.

You can take good fish in the mountain streams at surprisingly high altitudes as long as the stream has enough water and the gradient isn't too steep, but even steep pocket water can be deceptive. A lot of fishermen want to fish the flats and pools in a stream, and a fast, rocky, mountain creek can look rather uninviting. This kind of water can, however, hide some beautiful trout habitat and the fish to go with it.

In most high mountain pocket water you're looking at fish that will top out at about ten or twelve inches, with enough smaller ones to give you the feeling that those are the big fish, which they usually are. If you take one that goes closer to fourteen inches, you've probably caught the biggest old mossback in the whole stream, and you should stop and toast your luck, skill, or whatever else you think was responsible before you release him.

This is probably not the kind of water you should seek out if you're a big fish hunter, but it can provide fast, active fishing for bright, strong, healthy trout. I don't think that takes a backseat to any other kind of fly-fishing.

Another thing about the small, high streams is the fish you find there will almost invariably be "home growns." Many of the high lakes, not to mention the lower streams and rivers, are periodically stocked with hatchery fish, but the little mountain streams are seldom if ever stocked. Although these fish are often the *products* of stocking somewhere along the drainage, the small stream trout was, nine times out of ten, born and raised right there where you caught him.

To my mind, the dry fly is king in pocket water, both because nymphs and streamers are often next to impossible to fish and because the trout will tend to be fast and aggressive and can often be easily lured to the surface. Some of the high streams serve up fine heavy hatches of mayflies, caddis, and even stoneflies, but in most cases it's not necessary to match these bugs very closely with your fly patterns, although notable exceptions to that rule are not completely unknown.

A case in point: I was coming out of a little canyon that I'd been fishing for most of the afternoon, fishing downstream but moving pretty fast trying to get back out to the car by nightfall so that I wouldn't break my neck scrambling over the boulders in the dark. As usual, I was fishing a #14 Humpy. I came to a little pool out in the middle of the fast water, no bigger than, say, the hood of an American car, with some trout rising in it. There were three or four of them, and one looked pretty good.

I popped my Humpy in there, got a decent drift, and tensed for the strike that I was sure would come. In fact, I'd have bet a dollar on getting a hit, but it didn't come on the first cast and it hadn't come by the fifth. Okay, I thought, they want me to get fancy—so I tied on a #20 Adams and repeated the performance.

By this time it was getting dark and the larger fish had stopped rising, but his smaller friends were still at it. I crawled down to the tail of the pool—keeping low so as not to spook the trout—and looked in the water, which was well-covered with #16 Red Quill spinners lying with their wings flat on the surface, spent after (probably) mating over the riffle at the head of the little pool.

A standard #16 Red Quill dry didn't work either, and a badly dragging float put down another fish. I had no spinners, so I made a rough one by pulling the wings from my dry fly and clipping the hackle top and bottom to get the fly right down in the surface film the way the naturals were. The fish I finally hooked and landed was a six-inch cutthroat, but he'd been as selective as a spring creek brown and I was very pleased with myself. I also now carry some spinners on the mountain creeks.

Under normal conditions, though, I prefer highly visible flies for pocket water—patterns like the Royal Humpy with its white calf hair wings or the light Elk Hair Caddis—that I can see in fast water. I've tried matching the bugs more accurately on a regular basis, but I just have too much trouble keeping my eyes on something like a #16 Red Quill in fast water. A Royal Humpy may, in fact, draw fewer strikes, but I can *see* the takes and so I hook more fish—a fair bargain, I think.

Someone once referred to pocket water fishing as "picking pockets," and that's a perfect description. The fish will typically hold in spots where they're out of the main currents

Fishing pocket water in a high country stream.

but close enough to them so they'll be able to see, and grab at, the insects that go by. These spots don't have to be very big—just big enough to hold a fish. You'll find them behind rocks, against logs, along cut banks, and in current eddies along the bends in the stream. In pocket water, anyplace that's a little calmer or slower than the rest of the current is worth a cast or two.

One thing I always look for in a situation like this is the foam line—the place where a faster and a slower current slide up against one another and things collect, like sticks, bubbles, and floating bugs. Sometimes these are easy to spot and sometimes they're not, but they're excellent spots for a trout to look for trapped bugs that he doesn't have to spend a lot of energy to get. Rises in foam lines are often very, *very* subtle and hard to detect.

Foam lines are hard to cast to. For one thing, you'll probably pick up debris on your hook, and for another, a good drift can be maddening to try and pull off. It's best to fish them from the calmer side, but that will make it easier for the fish to see you. If you're on the fast side, you can get closer without being spotted, but it's always harder to cast from a fast current into a slower one. Often something like impenetrable brush or a sheer, forty-foot cliff on one side or the other will help you make the decision.

Also keep in mind that although some holding spots are so obvious they might as well have a sign over them reading "trout here," others can be downright invisible. When a trout comes out of nowhere in fast water, I think it's because his calm holding spot is on the bottom, say behind a football-sized rock that breaks the current. This sort of thing is more likely to happen in shallow water than deep, but it's a good idea to run a few casts over the fast riffles, just to see what happens. This is especially effective in riffles where the bottom is heavily cobbled wth big rocks. Remember that you're working in two dimensions when casting a dry fly on the surface of a stream but the trout is working in three dimensions. I've seen some very good trout taken in the kind of fast, shallow water that many fishermen pass by on their way to the pools and slicks.

Probably the thing that's most consistently difficult about pocket water is getting a good, drag-free float. Even an aggressive pocket water trout will refuse a fly that drags, and once he's turned away from it, it's hard to get him to come back, even if you get the drag out on the next few casts. Even if a Humpy doesn't look much like a real bug, it's got to *act* like a real bug. One thing that will sometimes work is to simply change flies. Go to something in the same size but of a different pattern once you've worked out a good float with the fly that was refused.

Fast, conflicting currents can play hell with your line and leader, causing that fatal drag. The best way to avoid this is to fish a short cast and keep as much line off the water as possible. Luckily, the same conditions that make a dead drift

A trout on in a mountain stream. The tails of pools like this are often good.

so difficult will also cover your approach and your cast fairly well, allowing you to get in close.

In many situations with fast, conflicting currents, the only possible dead drift is at the end of a downstream cast. Here you get upstream of a rising fish or a good lie, drop the fly on a slack line above the desired spot, and let it drift down. Ideally, you should be in such a position that the rod tip is right above the current in which your fly is floating, something that seems to be possible about 50 percent of the time.

The main problem with the downstream dry fly float is that, although it often gives the best presentation of the fly in fast water, it also presents the worst possible hooking angle. When a trout takes a fly from the surface, he will either open his mouth, flare his gill covers, and suck it in—along with a little air or water— from underneath, or he'll do the same thing while he sort of rolls on the fly. The latter is often called a head and tail rise.

Now if you're downstream of the fish (at his back) when he does this, your strike will pull the fly back into his mouth, but if you're upstream, you'll be pulling it out. For this reason, a strike on a downstream float usually requires a slight hesitation, just enough time for the fish to close his mouth and turn. How long a hesitation? It will probably vary a little every day of your life, depending on the individual trout, the stream in question, your own current reaction time (how well you slept last night), and who knows what else. It also takes nerves of steel until you get used to it, but don't forget to hesitate. When most of us start missing strikes, we think we're striking too slow; it seldom occurs to us that we're not slow *enough*.

Another way to get a drag-free float in conflicting currents is to use a pile cast, which is just what it sounds like: a cast where your leader—and maybe even part of your line—piles back in coils that are pulled out by the current while the fly, theoretically, drifts perfectly for a few seconds. It's a good cast for those times when you have to work a slow current on the far side of a fast one, and it's pretty easy to pull off. In fact, it's one of the mistakes we all made when we we're learning to cast a fly rod.

You simply stop the cast too high over the water, and the recoil from the force of the cast pulls the line and leader back on itself. You can enhance the effect by pulling the rod sharply back toward you at just about the time the line straightens out. A good caster can pile a twelve-foot leader in a space no larger than a dinner plate. My friend Archie (A.K.) Best judges pile casts by the number of times the fly bobs freely in the slack water before the current takes up the slack and it streams out of there, leaving a wake like a motorboat, as in "I think I can get a four bob float over there."

I only use a pile cast when there's no other choice, because one of two things will invariably happen. The trout will either rise to the fly the instant the slack goes out and he'll refuse it as it starts to drag, or he'll take it the instant it hits the water and you've got so much slack out that you couldn't set the hook if your arms were twelve feet long. Still, if all else fails, it's worth a try on a good fish in a hard spot.

Each spot will, naturally, present a unique casting problem. You may want to make your delivery upstream, across, or straight down. On rare occasions you may even want to get out of the water altogether and dap your fly.

Dapping is an old English trick that involves nothing more than fishing just a few feet of leader past the tip-top guide and setting your fly on the water directly under the end of the rod. Obviously, problems of drag are eliminated, and you can even make your fly bounce up and down on the surface like a freshly hatched natural trying to take off. The main problem is concealing yourself, and dapping is best done while lying on the bank on your stomach or hiding in a bush. Regardless of how well you're hidden, the appearance of that rod over the surface will usually spook trout in still or shallow water.

I could go on about this with example after example, but I believe that pocket water and small stream casting are among those skills you learn in the field through experience, not from a book. A good stream will provide hundreds of opportunities in a mile, and it seldom does any good to work a spot for very long anyway. Keep moving, keep casting, and don't be afraid to experiment.

The ancient Chinese philosophers used the qualities of water to illustrate what human enlightenment should be like. Water is completely passive, it takes on whatever characteristics its environment requires, and it thereby becomes the most powerful element in nature—a neat idea and an accurate observation. A fast mountain stream will become a gentle glide wherever the terrain allows and spots like this are usually the best trout habitat. All things being equal, trout will tend to be larger in meadow sections, side channels, backwaters, and anywhere else where they don't have to work as hard for their food.

These fish will probably still be opportunistic most of the time, but they'll also probably be a little more cautious because they have more time to examine what they bite and because the quieter water lets them see better and farther into our element. I usually fish a short leader with about a 4x tippet in faster water, but I'll almost always go to a longer and at least slightly finer one in quiet sections. If I decide to stay with a dry fly, I'll go to a more realistic pattern, like an Adams, or at least a smaller Humpy.

If trout are ever going to be spooky and selective in the high country streams, it's most likely to happen in these quieter sections for the simple reason that conditions permit it. A quiet stretch is also an excellent candidate for a good, steady rise for the same reason. This doesn't mean that you can't pound fish up to a general pattern. In fact, this can be very productive when no particular insect activity is going on. During mid to late summer, at the lower altitudes where the natural bugs are in evidence, a grasshopper fly is an excellent search pattern that can bring up the big fish. Higher up where grasshoppers seldom go, you're better off with a Humpy, Adams, or caddis pattern.

If you can see fish rising or working just under the surface, it's not unusual to get strikes to an attractor pattern, but it's always worth the time to take a few minutes and watch first before you just barge in. It's been my experience that if the feeding activity is to something like a hatch of Speckled Spinners in a size 18 and you try a #12 Humpy, you'll get strikes, but not from the larger fish. The bigger fish will often be at least slightly more selective to something that looks a little bit more like the real thing, with size being much more crucial than color or shape.

Another way to get the larger fish is to *find them and cast to them*, another good reason for watching the water for a while before making that all-important first cast. During a rise, you can often spot the good fish by their rise forms, but don't always count on that. Sometimes a very large trout can make a very small dimple on the surface, especially when he's taking something that's small and/or inactive, like mayfly

Working the tail of a pool in a small stream.

spinners or spent flying ants. If all the rises look to be about the same size, look for the one that seems to move the most water behind it.

During a heavy hatch, good fish will probably be in the most ideal spot for feeding, and that usually means right where the fast water comes into the pool or somewhere along the edge of that current, although at times they will also lie at the tail of the pool. When the hatch is sparse and the activity is less than what you'd call frantic, look for the bigger fish along the banks and out of—but near—the main currents.

By the way, trout that appear to be feeding on the surface to hatching insects but who refuse your flies may, in fact, be taking emergers from just under the surface. If your dry fly hasn't produced—and you haven't spooked the fish—try a floating nymph.

Often the larger fish, in fast water or slow, will choose to feed on or near the bottom, both during a hatch and when things are slow. The way to get a fly down to these deep feeders is to add a little weight to your leader about fifteen to twenty inches above the fly. Some people like split shot, while others prefer Twist-ons. Split shot has the advantage of being reusable, but Twist-ons will not slide around on the leader as much.

With small amounts of lead you can cast some distance and follow your drift by watching the floating portion of your line or leader. With a heavy rig, flip the weighted fly upstream from where you think the fish will be holding, and let it sink. Strip in line so there's only enough slack to ensure a realistic, drag-free drift of the nymph, and follow the drift with your rod tip.

The strike to a deep-drifted nymph is likely to be very subtle and is usually signaled by nothing more than a little twitch, jiggle, bounce, or hesitation in the line. Naturally, your line will be doing this more or less constantly as your weight ticks on the bottom, but the really good nymph fishermen I know set at *any* indication of a strike, no matter how subtle or questionable. For some reason, this doesn't seem to spook fish as easily as if you were constantly ripping a dry fly from the surface.

Patterns? Something general and buggy-looking, like a Hare's Ear Soft Hackle or a Zug Bug, in a size 12 or 14, is good for searching. During a hatch, it's best to try to roughly match the size of the insects that are coming off.

Trout seldom suspend at mid-depths. If they're feeding deep (or just holding and waiting for something to come along), they'll be right on the bottom, so use enough weight to get your fly down deep and don't be surprised if you hang a few on the bottom. If you don't, you're not fishing deep enough.

If a dead-drifted nymph doesn't work, try giving the fly a little action. You can do this by either raising the fly off the bottom slightly with the rod tip or letting it swing up downstream. This can be especially effective during a hatch when some fish may be keyed on the action of the rising nymphs or pupae. But remember to impart *a little* action. The most common tendency here is to be too heavy-handed.

Slow, mellow glides and fast pocket water are the two extremes, but there are infinite variations in between. As a general rule, the slower the current and the deeper the water, the better a stream will be, and a high country stream changes with the lay of the land, sometimes drastically and suddenly. A steep little stream that crashes down a slope may well be worth investigating if a map or a friend tells you that it widens into a meadow a mile or two upstream. Tips and hunches like that are worth following up, because a hidden half mile of beautiful water along a little creek that no one fishes will likely stay hidden.

It's surprising how a small piece of a small stream can be good when most of it is largely uninteresting. The first few hundred yards of a stream as it flows into or out of a good lake can be excellent, better than the lake at times, especially in the late afternoons and in the mornings when the fish may move into the current to feed. In some cases, a good-sized channel will connect two high lakes, and these can be wonderful, even though they may be much higher than you'd expect a stream that big to be.

Some of the great sleepers among high streams are the channels between beaver ponds. Not only will a string of beaver ponds vastly improve the former stream habitat at the ponds themselves, but the stream connecting them will often be deep and slow. Many anglers prefer to hop from pond to pond in places like this, and that's another advantage to the channels: any place that other anglers tend to leave alone is worth a shot.

Many anglers also pass up the brushiest, hardest-to-reach sections of high streams (and low streams, for that matter), and these are often worth trying unless you have a very short fuse. There may well be a nice fish in the middle of a fifty-yard brush tunnel on a little creek—especially if there's a good looking hole—but you can lose a lot of flies trying to find out. I've tried very short rods for this kind of situation, but a five-and-one-half-foot fly rod is almost useless for anything else and you'll go mad if you fish spots like this all day. Now I satisfy my curiousity by feeding a small streamer or wet fly downstream.

It's like I said at the beginning—high country streams are like trout streams anywhere except they're usually smaller. They're also usually a little easier to fish from a matching the hatch standpoint and a little to a lot harder to fish from a technical standpoint because of their reduced scale. And again, like all trout streams, they're fascinating.

Cutthroat trout.

The Fish

ONCE UPON A TIME, DIFFERENT areas of the country had their own indigenous species of cold-water gamefish, and that was that. We human beings have changed that, the way we seem to want to change everything, and, with the fish as with everything else, sometimes we've done well and other times we've really screwed up.

Though some populations of native trout still exist and some others have been re-introduced, many of the fish we take in the mountain waters were introduced from other parts of the country. In many cases, the introduction of foreign species has contributed to the decline of native trout populations that couldn't compete with the new fish, and in other cases, it has established fish where there were none before. Many of our high country lakes and streams, especially those at the highest altitudes and/or behind natural barriers, were without fish a hundred years ago, and it's probably safe to say there are more fish in the western mountains now than there were then. All things considered, I think I can live with that.

Many fishermen have a soft spot in their hearts for their own native fish, and I'm no exception. Here in Colorado, as in most interior Western States, native means cutthroat. The original range of the various species and subspecies of cutthroats extends down the west coast from Alaska to California and throughout the Mountain West in the United States and Canada. In coastal areas they will run to sea like steelhead.

As you go through the reference books, it seems as though every major river drainage—and a few minor ones—evolved its own subspecie of cutthroat, which was named, in many cases, for the river: Yellowstone, Colorado River, Rio Grande, Snake River, and so on. There are also a lot of local names, and any cutthroat that you can think of has been, at one time or another, referred to as a "speckled trout."

The various subspecies of cutthroat will readily interbreed with each other and, in many cases, with the rainbow trout. So there are a lot of "generic" cutthroats around—the products of stocking, say, the Yellowstone cutt in a Snake-River-cutt stream—and there are also a lot of cuttbows, or rainbow/cutthroat crosses. Pure strains of some of the more obscure subspecies of cutt are now considered rare, endangered, or, in some cases, extinct.

This state of affairs can be blamed on destruction of habitat in somes cases, on improper stocking of introduced species in others, and sometimes, as in the case of the Lahonton cutthroat—a trout that was once caught in sizes to rival the Atlantic salmon—on a combination of abuses like heavy commercial fishing and the destruction of spawning areas.

Cutthroats exhibit considerable variation in color and spotting pattern, but they are basically an olive green trout—often with a hint of yellow or bronze—with black spots, the "cutthroat" red slash under the lower jaws, and, often, reddish or orange gill covers. The spotting pattern is distinctive. It may involve roughly uniform small black pepper spots as in the Snake River cutt, large dark spots distributed mostly toward the rear as in the Rio Grande cutt, or almost anything in between, depending on the specie or the mix.

Cutthroats are pretty trout, and it seems as though they're just a little bit different in every piece of water—a few more spots in one lake than another, a little more yellow or a little more green on the sides—but I've never paid much attention to the strict taxonomic differences. If someone says to me "big cutts," I don't ask "what kind?" I ask "where?"

I got excited about learning to distinguish between the various cutthroats and crosses, but I soon ran into more science than I could handle. To give you an idea of what you're up against here, I'll quote a fairly typical passage from *The Native Trouts of the Genus* Salmo *of Western North America* by Robert J. Behnke:

> "The Colorado River Cutthroat trout and the greenback cutthroat trout consistently exhibit the highest scale counts of any of the subspecies, with the possible exception of *S. c. alpestris.* Lateral series scale counts range from 170 to well over 200. Pure populations of *pleuriticus* should average more than 180 scales in the lateral series and more than 43 scales above the lateral line. Vertebrae numbers typically range from 60 to 63, with mean values of about 61 or 62. Gillraker numbers range from 17 to 21, with mean values of about 19."

Now I'm not making fun of this. In fact, I quoted Dr. Behnke because he is considered by many to be *the* authority on the cutthroat trout. My point is that I don't think many of us are prepared to dissect our trout for the purpose of exact identification. I don't even kill very many, and those that I do go right into the frying pan with their scales and gillrakers uncounted. Exact identification of species and subspecies should probably be left to people who understand that quote, and the rest of us should just be happy to be catching "cutthroats." For obvious reasons, I won't be bringing up subtle taxonomic features in the rest of this discussion.

Technically, the brook trout isn't a trout at all; it's a char—a close relative. It's the rare fisherman who makes the distinction, though. The brookie is native to the East Coast of North America, originally ranging as far north as the Arctic

Brook trout.

Circle and as far south as what is now Georgia, though they've been introduced almost everywhere now with varying degrees of success.

The problem with brook trout is they tend to overpopulate the waters where they've been introduced. Some say this is because they evolved in predator-filled environments and reproduced heavily as a defense mechanism. Then, when they're put in predator-free waters, their populations explode. Others will tell you that it's the brookie's short life span—maybe three or four years in some areas—plus the fact that they can spawn in habitat that would be marginal to unacceptable for other species.

Many, perhaps even most, of the mountain brook trout waters are filled with stunted fish, but there are certain situations, like a new beaver pond or a significant lack of spawning area, that will grow big ones. When brookies get big, fishermen often start calling them brook "trout," a term that exhibits a little more respect.

A big brook trout is a real prize, and one of the reasons is because they're so pretty. The typical brookie has a two-tone olive back with wormlike markings that shade to amber, pink, or red on the lower sides and white on the belly. The lower fins are pink to orange with white leading edges, and the spots are red with blue haloes, usually against a background of yellowish mottling. There's a good deal of color variation, but the brightest fish seem to come, for some reason, from beaver ponds.

Rainbows are special favorites of hatchery managers and are probably the most likely trout to be stocked, especially on a put-and-take basis. They're often found in the high country in the more accessible lakes and streams. The rainbows exhibit wide variations in coloration, but the typical fish is greenish-olive on the back, shading to silvery sides and a whitish belly. The distinctive pink to red rainbow stripe extends down the lateral line. The fish will have small black spots, usually heavier toward the top and back.

The rainbow is native to the West Coast of North America where the steelhead is the sea-run form.

Hatchery rainbows are sometimes referred to by fishermen as "sickies" or "dummies" and it's true that many domestic strains of rainbow seem slow and stupid when compared to their wild relatives. I don't believe I've ever caught rainbows that were truly native, but I've fished over ones that have held over from the original stocking, sometimes for generations, and have long since forgotten their roots in the concrete runs of a hatchery.

The cuttbow—the rainbow/cutthroat—is common in some high country waters, and they can be fine fish. Sometimes the crossbreeding is evident, and you'll catch something with the characteristic cutthroat slashes that otherwise looks to be a rainbow. In other cases, so I'm told, you'll take what appear to be cutthroats, and only a trained biologist could tell they weren't pure strain.

It's been said that the cuttbow (not to mention the presence of brook trout in waters where they don't seem to belong) is the result of improper stocking procedures, but that may not be entirely fair. The simple facts are that fisheries managers didn't always know as much as they do now and that, in many cases, the experts were not in control of which fish were put where. I've been told that some of the early stocking programs in Colorado involved bringing tank cars of fingerlings to railheads, where local folks could get a bucket or a milk can full and put them wherever they pleased, on the premise that lots of fish are better than a few—even if the few were big, native cutts.

The distinction between native and wild fish is an interesting one. Some of the introduced species have established themselves and have been successfully reproducing in the West for decades. Sad to say, there are probably more "wild" populations of introduced fish than there are self-sustaining populations of our own natives.

A biologist with the U.S. Fish and Game Service told me once that he came upon the records from the very first trout hatchery in Colorado. He thought he might be able to find out exactly when the brook trout arrived out here—something that apparently no one is really clear about. But it seems that on their first full day of operation, they went out and caught wild brookies as brood stock for the hatchery.

All wild trout are pretty to look at, with color combinations that you could never decorate your living room in but that look just fine on a live fish in a mountain lake. But the golden trout is probably the most beautiful of them all. The golden has an overall yellowish color with an olive back, often with red highlights on the gill covers, lateral line, and lower fins. Goldens retain their parr marks (large oval spots along the sides) throughout their lives, while other trout lose them as they mature. According to A.J. McClane's *Standard Fishing Encyclopedia*, the golden was originally found in the headwaters of California's Kern River. However, these fine fish have been introduced into the high country waters in several western states. The world record golden was taken from the Bridger Wilderness Area in Wyoming, and, by all accounts, that area still represents the best opportunity for a large specimen.

Grayling are special favorites of mine, probably because they're so rare in my part of the country. Grayling originated in the north country (Alaska and the Northwest Territories), and their native range apparently extended as far south as parts of Montana and Michigan. They've been introduced into several western mountain states where they seem to do just fine in the cold, high lakes. However, in many cases where reproduction occurs, they will stunt themselves like brook trout.

Some trout fishers look down their noses at grayling—I've even heard the fish referred to as glorified whitefish—but they are pretty fish that come to a fly well, and it doesn't bother me at all that they aren't trout.

The scientific name for grayling is *Thymallus tricolor* because of the coloration and the fact that the fish is supposed to smell like thyme—something I've never noticed. The fish are trout-shaped with a distinctive high dorsal fin that's spotted in iridescent blues and purples. This dorsal fin is used in mating displays, and I believe the fish also uses it when fighting with a fisherman. On a trip to the Northwest Territories a few years ago, the best fight I had was from a two-and-one-half-pound grayling that turned sideways like a bluegill in the fast current of the Kazan River. He flared that fin and peeled the line and half the backing from my light reel.

A typical grayling is silvery in color—often with a bronze, olive, or blue cast—with a darker back and a few dark spots sprinkled toward the front of the body.

Grayling can be hard to hook, and the myth has developed that they have "soft mouths." In fact, their mouths are hard enough—the hooking problem comes from the fact that they will often roll on a fly, coming out of the water next to it and taking it on the way down. Speaking from experience, I can say that it's easy to strike too soon and either miss the fish, or only nick him and it *does* feel like the mouth is soft.

When fishing for grayling with dry flies, it's usually necessary to hesitate on the strike. It takes a little getting used to, but it works. Trout will strike like that too at times but not usually on a regular basis like grayling.

I won't say a lot about brown trout because they are seldom found in the high country. But there are some exceptions (there are *always* exceptions), so I suppose they rate a little space here.

Browns were introduced into this country from Europe just about 100 years ago, and they are, along with the ringneck pheasant and the English sparrow, among the most successful of the transplanted species. They are an overall golden brown color with black and red spots and often have a bluish cast on the gill covers and down the sides. When you see them flash in the water, they look to be about the color of butter. To my eye, they are the most tastefully colored of all the trout.

Browns will now and then work their way into high country streams from lakes and reservoirs where they've been stocked, and there may be year-around populations in some of the lower mountain streams. In their normal, low-altitude habitat range, browns are heavy fish eaters, but there's some debate as to whether they will carry that habit into the mountains with them.

It's been suggested by some anglers that browns in a brook trout fishery will get big from eating the little brookies and will also increase the size of the brook trout by keeping their numbers down. I don't know if that's true or not—I know of waters that seem to bear that out and others that seem to contradict it. Two things I *do* know: browns are especially susceptible to streamer patterns (little fish imitations), and any brown trout water sooner or later usually yields up a really big brown—quite often to a kid with a stick, string, and gob of worms.

Browns and brook trout are fall spawners, while cutthroats, rainbows, goldens, and grayling all spawn in the spring,

though even approximate dates are hard to figure because
spring and fall are such relative terms in the high country.
A high lake with both brookies and cutts may have spawning
activity going on for almost the entire season.

According to most biologists, all of these fish—with the
possible exception of mature browns—feed almost entirely
on insects and crustaceans when they're found in the high
country waters, and the fact that any high country trout or
grayling may now and then nail a streamer does not
necessarily refute that. I don't claim to know how trout think
or even if they think at all, but I wouldn't be surprised to
learn that they grab a streamer (*when* they grab a streamer)
not because they believe it to be a little fish, but just because
they're curious. I do, however, believe that trout will eat
leeches in lakes where these unpleasant creatures are
common, if only because a small black Wooly Bugger can be
such a deadly pattern in a leech lake.

You'll often see personality profiles of the various trout or
hear them alluded to, as in "he came out from under the
bank and slammed it like a brown." You'll be told that browns
are shy and selective with a vicious predatory streak, that
brookies are stupid and aggressive, and that the others fall
somewhere in between. These ideas have grown up as
matters of tradition, and they're largely accurate in a regional
kind of way. But broad statements about how specific kinds
of fish act aren't all that useful to the high country fly
fisherman.

I believe that trout are like people in that their behavior is
determined largely by their environment. If I'd been raised
in the slums of a big city—which I wasn't—I might not be
the easygoing nice guy I am today. A brown trout, shy and
selective as he's supposed to be, who's raised in a small,
sparse creek, will be as aggressive and opportunistic as any
brook trout. That, I think, applies to all trout waters, not just
those in the high country. In secluded waters where food is
relatively scarce and life is tough, the fish will tend toward
opportunistic feeding habits. In heavily fished waters with

large populations of insects and regular, heavy hatches, they will probably be spooky and selective, regardless of what kind of fish they happen to be.

Some anglers like to characterize selective trout as "smart" and aggressive fish, like high lake brookies, as "dumb," but I think it's exactly the other way around. If you act like a selective trout the next time you go to a restaurant, you'll start nibbling on the breadsticks and, having determined they're good to eat, you'll ignore your spaghetti when it comes because you don't recognize it as food. That's not smart.

The high country trout, having learned from his harsh, sparse environment, will feed steadily on midges if that's all there is, but he'll also stop for a minute and grab a big caddis pupa that happens to swim by.

I don't mean to discount the stereotypes entirely, though, because they hold some truth. If browns and rainbows are in the same stream, the rainbows are almost invariably easier to catch on a day-to-day basis, and that fits the profile. Grayling, rainbows, and brook trout are, in fact, a bit easier to take on attractors, and cutthroats and goldens *do* have a shy, retiring streak.

Then there's the interesting fact that the behavior of any given population of trout will change from season to season, day to day, even hour to hour. Sometimes the reasons for this are obvious (changes in weather, time of day, food availability), and sometimes the reasons are known only to the fish themselves.

Still, I'll stand by my statement. Trout behavior is dictated largely by the habitat in which the fish are living, and there are many more similarities between the species of trout and grayling than there are differences. If you're going to fish a piece of water with any preconceived ideas, base them on the type of habitat and not the kind of fish.

A selection of soft hackled wet flies.

Tackle and Flies

QUESTIONS ABOUT WHAT KIND of tackle and flies to use in various situations have kept a whole raft of magazine editors, fishing writers, manufacturers, fly tiers, and tackle dealers fed for many years. It's easy to get bogged down with more gear than you need, especially since most of the fly fishermen I know are born packrats, but that's exactly what you don't want to do when you're fishing the high country. The simplest and lightest setup that still fills your needs is the best.

The length, line weight, and material for the ideal fly rod are subjects of heated and ongoing debates—friendly ones, for the most part—and, like all debates that are based on one personal preference over another, they'll probably never be settled. If by some chance they are, some manufacturer will come out with a rod made of some new space-age material and start the whole thing over again. Remember when graphite was new?

It's also easy to get caught up in the idea that you need a bunch of specialized rods for different conditions and kinds of fishing, and, although it's true that a dedicated flyfisher might "need" a light, a medium, and a heavy rod, some of us take it to extremes. How about a 7-foot 3-weight for those little, shallow beaver ponds on calm clear days, a 7½-foot

4-weight for the same ponds on cloudy days and for the small streams, an 8-foot 5-weight for bigger streams and bigger ponds, an 8½-foot 5-weight for a little more punch (longer casts or more wind), a 9-foot 5-weight for light work on lakes, and a 9-foot 6-weight for a little more punch (again)? How about a 10-foot 7-weight for big, windy lakes? I'm not being condescending here—those are some of my rods.

Then there's the material to consider: fiberglass, graphite, or split cane. Fiberglass is the cheapest by far, and a good glass rod will perform much better than some would have you believe. All they lack is the real power for the outlandishly long casts that most of us don't need to make more than four or five times a season anyway—casts that most of us couldn't make regardless of what kind of rod we were holding.

Graphite *has* that power, and it's also lighter and smaller in diameter than a comparable glass rod, although I sometimes think that too much is made of the weight difference. When you're talking about fractions of an ounce, how much difference can it make? I don't think the reduced wind resistance from the slightly smaller diameter is a big deal, either.

Apparently it's possible to make a graphite rod with a fairly slow action, but graphite seems to be a rather stiff material, and most of the popular rods are what you'd have to call fast action. I like that, and it's a good action to have for dry fly fishing and for medium to long casting. The only graphite rods I really like are the long ones, nine feet and better, because this is where the material seems to do its job best. The short rods seem to me to be either too soft and whippy (so why bother with graphite?) or so stiff they won't cushion light tippets.

I've been a split cane freak for quite a while now, so I'm going to push my favorite material at the expense of the others. It's interesting that the word expense popped up there, because the cost of cane rods puts them out of the reach of many flyfishers. It's hard to say whether a cane fly rod is acutally "worth," say, $850, but if that's what it costs and you buy it, then it was worth it to you. At least that's how I understand economics.

Cane, being an organic material, is harder to work with than the synthetics, and that's what makes the rods more expensive. But they have an unmistakable heft and feel that's hard to do without once you get used to it. On the practical side, it seems to me that cane rods have smoother, more forgiving actions than most synthetic rods, and, although they may be an instant slower on the strike than a stiff graphite, they'll do a much better job of cushioning a light tippet against the runs and head shakings of a big trout.

Cane rods are heavier than graphite, and that can be a problem in the longer lengths and heavier line weights. I have a very nice 9-foot 7-weight cane that I just don't fish anymore because it's too heavy—makes my elbow sore by the end of the day. On the shorter 4-and 5-weight rods, however, I find the extra heft comfortable and pleasant. I can feel the rod load better and don't always have to be looking over my shoulder (as I tend to do with light graphites) to see where my back cast is going.

My own personal preference is for my lighter, shorter rods to be cane and my longer, heavier ones to be graphite. That way both materials are beng used to their greatest advantage. I'm not exactly sure where the breaking point is, but I'd say that an 8-foot 6-weight could go either way.

Like I said, cane rods are a personal preference for me. I like them as much for their feeling of class and tradition as anything else, and it should be obvious that I'm speaking as a user of rods, not as a designer or engineer. If I ever decided to spend my money more wisely, those shorter, lighter rods would be fiberglass.

Some high country flyfishers and backpackers like a four-piece pack rod that can be slipped into the pack, leaving your hands free. The main criticism of pack rods is that the extra ferrules tend to deaden the action, and I think that's true when you're dealing with the long metal ferrules that you'll find on cane and older glass rods. Most modern pack rods, however, have ferrules made from the same material as the blank itself (fiberglass or graphite) and are not, as far as I can tell, noticeably different from comparable two-piece rods.

I don't own a pack rod myself and I never have. I have enough rods already. I've always just carried a two-piece rod in its case and I've never had any trouble with it. If you're like me, you'll be tempted to use the case as a walking stick at times, and that's fine as long as the rod is in a cloth bag and the case is padded top and bottom with a piece of foam. I would only do this with a good, solid, aluminum case, and I use it as a walking stick, not as a crutch or a club.

Some fishermen who do a lot of horse packing have told me they like four-piece rods because they don't stick out from the pack frame, where they could get caught on rocks or trees. But for the most part, I think a pack rod in a short case is most valuable to the guy who wants to take a fly rod along on his next business trip and doesn't want to advertise it.

What it all comes down to is there may be, for you, a perfect rod for a given lake or pond, but there is no overall perfect rod for general high country fishing, especially since it's not at all uncommon to fish a tiny beaver pond, a small creek, and a big lake on the same trip. If I'm going to a particular spot, I'll take the rod that I think will suit that spot best, but on a more extended trip (or one where I don't quite know where I'll end up), I take a 9-foot graphite for a #5 or #6 line.

Most high country conditions call for a floating fly line. I prefer the double taper lines because I think they cast better under a variety of conditions and because you can turn them around when one end wears out and have what amounts to a brand new fly line. Looked at another way, it's like getting two for the price of one.

Many anglers now prefer the weight forward lines, and these have some advantages. You can shoot more line because more weight goes out quicker (although this doesn't necessarily mean that you can cast farther), and they will load a rod with less line out. As a result, they can be a bit easier for very short casts, like on a little stream. Still, I think the double taper is the better all-around line, and it is certainly the better bargain.

If you're going to be fishing a lake of any size, it's a good idea to carry a spare spool loaded with a sink-tip line. Sink-tip lines come with heads of varying lengths and densities, but for most high lake work, a ten-foot, medium sink-tip is about right.

A sink-tip is the best and often the only way to adequately fish nymphs, wet flies, or streamers in more than about four feet of still water. This isn't something you'll find yourself doing very often, but on those occasions when you need it, you'll kick yourself if it's back home in the desk drawer. A spare spool is better than a whole spare reel because it helps keep the weight down.

When it comes to fly patterns, I have the same unreasonable fear as most fly fishers: that of being caught without the correct fly pattern or, worse yet, having only one and losing it. I even had a screaming nightmare about it. The guy I was with thought I was being eaten by a bear.

I've already said that high country trout and grayling are *usually* not selective but that there are exceptions to the rule. That's an easy statement to make until you start trying to develop a small, compact fly selection.

My high country fly selection changes from year to year as I decide to add patterns that have caught my eye and take those out that I haven't caught a fish on in recent memory. Every winter I go through it to get ready for the coming spring, and, with a nucleus of a few patterns that never change, I start more or less at the beginning.

I can usually safely eliminate the bass bugs and the 2/0 pike streamers, but when I get much past that, the old caught-without-the-right-pattern paranoia kicks in. Can I get along without the #8 Royal Wulffs? The fact that I've never caught a fish on one in my life should probably be taken into consideration.

Something else that should be taken into consideration is the fact that no two fly fishermen carry and catch fish on the same patterns, even those who fish the same water—

something I've written off as one of life's little mysteries. So I'm going to list my current high country fly selection—not so you'll copy it, but to try and illustrate the logic (if that's the word) that has gone into it.

I wouldn't feel dressed without the Hare's Ear Soft Hackle (weighted) in sizes 10 through 16. It's a nondescript, fuzzy, buggy-looking fly that will pass for just about any aquatic insect depending on how you fish it. I have a special affection for this pattern because I thought I invented it (not so, it turns out), but I can still say I've taken the majority of my high lake fish on it.

Next to the Hares Ear Soft Hackles are the Zug Bugs. A Zug Bug is made almost entirely of peacock herl and has a buggy flash in the water that a cruising trout or grayling seems to just *have* to investigate. I carry them in sizes 10 through 16.

Fish in high lakes with a lot of freshwater shrimp will often get very selective to these crustaceans, so I also carry a shell-back shrimp pattern in gray, tan, and pink in sizes 12 through 16. Tan and gray are the two most common colors for shrimp that I've seen, but I've been thinking of adding an olive one for weedy lakes. Why the pink one? There are two theories. One is that when the shrimp molt, they turn pink for a while, and they're also most available to the fish at these times. The other is that the pink shrimp fly is just an eye-catcher—an attractor. Whatever, it works.

Midges are common on many high country waters, and the fish will often prefer the pupae over the winged flies, either fished deep or on or near the surface. I carry a light and a dark quill-bodied midge pupa in sizes 18 down to about 24, as well as a couple of dubbed-bodied olives and creams in the same sizes.

I also like to have an odd compartment full of assorted mayfly and caddis wets (numphs and pupae) just so I can change patterns after a refusal to one of the standards. Sometimes it makes a difference.

For dry flies I like the Adams, Humpy (or Royal Humpy with white wings), and a light and a dark Elk Hair Caddis.

These three will work as attractors and will also match a lot of common hatches adequately. The Humpys are in #10 through #18, Caddis about the same, and the Adams in #12 through #20.

As with the nymphs and wet flies, I also like to carry a few assorted mayflies,—mostly Blue Duns, Red Quills, and March Browns—in a variety of sizes for pattern changes and in anticipation of a hatch. Sizes are unusually about #14 down to #20 or #22.

There's also a compartment that's always filled with mayfly spinners, flying ants, and dry midge patterns. The spinners are simple darks and lights (chocolate brown and light cream), the ants are cinnamon and black, and the midges are cream, olive, and brown. Sizes 14 to 20 for the spinners, about the same for the ants, and #16 down to #24 for the midges. I've seldom had to go to these flies, but when I have, they were sorely needed.

I'll carry a few streamers—Muddler Minnows, Gray Squirrel Tails, and Black Leeches. Like the last batch, I don't use them often, but there have been times when I was very pleased I'd brought them. They're mostly in sizes 6 and 8, but the Squirrel Tail—nothing more than a silver tinsel body, gray squirrel wing, and a red head—goes down to a short shanked #10, at which point I suppose it's technically a fancy wet fly.

Those are the basic patterns that, at this writing at least, I feel are no less essential than a pair of pants on a mountain fishing expedition. I wish I could say they all fit neatly into a single fly box, but it's not so. I usually carry three.

So as not to appear more organized than I am, however, I should mention that I also like to carry other odd patterns. I usually have some big, bushy Flymphs (soft hackles with tails) in sizes 8 and 10 for deep, dark water, some small yellow grasshoppers, and maybe even some assorted bucktail streamers.

Finally, I will not go into the mountains to fish without a couple of Royal Coachman wet flies in sizes 12 and 14. That's right—the Royal Coachman. I can't imagine why a trout would bite a thing like that, but I became a believer one afternoon on a small stream in the Northern Rockies about ten years ago. I'd located a pod of good-looking cutthroats rising at the tail of a long, slow pool and, to keep a long story reasonable, fished every pattern in my box without either spooking them or getting so much as a glance at my fly. (I'll take that back—they casually moved out of the way of the streamers.)

Finally, more as an act of disrespect than anything else, I tied on a Royal Coachman wet that someone had given me and proceeded to take four fat trout between ten and fourteen inches. Since then I've repeated the performance often enough to be sold on the pattern but not often enough to have any idea why it works.

As I said, I don't expect anyone to take that as the last word on high country fly selections. For that matter, it may have changed a little by the time you read this. For instance, I'm thinking of adding the K.B. (Keith Bilby) Caddis Pupa after having had some success with it this summer. I know people who will yell at me for not including the Gray Hackle Yellow, the Breadcrust, the Black Gnat, and maybe the Hornburg. The point is, carry a variety of flies in different sizes and types.

One other thing. Don't ever carry just one fly of any pattern. If its turns out to be the one that works, you'll surely lose it. Carry no less than two of any pattern and size, preferably four or more.

Additional necessities can usually be pared down to a few spools of tippet material, maybe one or two spare full leaders in anticipation of the terminal wind knot, a set of clippers for trimming leader knots, a pair of forceps for removing hooks from fish and fishermen and for other odd chores, a bottle of fly floatant, and a small stone for sharpening hooks. I like to string all of this stuff together on a cord to keep it in one place.

How about a landing net? A landing net is one of those things that you don't often need, and the one time you *do* need it is the time you left it at home. I usually carry one.

There are some folding nets on the market, and, although I haven't tried all of them, I don't think much of them. If you're going to use one of these, don't carry it in its belt-loop holster and try some fancy, quick draw stuff in the final, crucial moments of landing a good fish. Open the thing up and hang it on your belt like a real net.

The single most useful thing that I've ever been able to do to reduce bulk and weight is to leave the fly vest at home and wear a "fishing shirt." In case you've never seen one, a fishing shirt is usually made of heavy cotton canvas with four big patch pockets on the front and a cargo pouch on the back. If you've kept your gear to a minimum, there's plenty of room for all of it, and the shirt takes up zero room in the pack because you're already wearing it. A fully loaded fly vest in a pack is about equal in size and weight to a day and a half's worth of food.

Then there's the question of waders. I think the best ones are the lightweight, stocking-foot chest waders that are on the market now. You'll get cold in them, and some of them tear easily if you're not careful, but they can be rolled up into a very small space and are relatively light.

Stocking-foot waders require wading boots, and these may be too big and heavy for an extended backpack. You can get around that by using a pair of light tennis shoes. You can even glue felt to the soles if you like; just make sure that you replace the cotton laces with nylon. The constant wetting and drying will rot the cotton laces in short order, and they will naturally break at the worst possible time. Also, make sure the tennis shoes fit over the wader feet and the extra socks you'll be wearing. Chances are that old pair of tennies in the closet will be too small.

I carry the waders, shoes, and heavy outside stockings in a big plastic bag that can be wrapped around several times and cinched up with rubber bands. On the trip back out, the shoes and socks will invariably be wet and the bag will keep water out of your clothes, gear, and cameras.

Any luxuries should be kept to a minimum, like a small flask of good whiskey and maybe a book. The whiskey is there for medicinal purposes, and the book is in case you have to spend nine hours in a tent waiting out a storm. Long, complicated historical novels are best.

All of this assumes a fairly long overnighter, where fishing gear, although of prime importance, has to be balanced against food, clothing, cooking utensils, and a bedroll, not to mention the natural enemy of the backpacker: weight. On one-day trips where you get into the stream a few hundred yards from the road or walk only a mile or so to a lake, it's not unreasonable to wear the vest and all its goodies and carry a pair of heavy-duty boot-foot waders. At times like that it's just too easy for me to stuff a sandwich and a candy bar in a pocket of the vest (along with the raincoat) and go, even though when I'm all geared up I weigh thirty pounds more than I'd have to. On longer trips, however, it's necessary to pare things down to a minimum. You'll travel easier, be more comfortable, and, if you go about it carefully and thoughtfully, you'll have everything you need.

Casting to the current at the head of a pond.

Prospecting

ALL THE TACTICS AND TECH-niques for fishing the high country lakes, streams, and beaver ponds make one critical assumption: that there are fish, preferably good ones, in the water. We like to think of the high country waters as wild, unspoiled places with populations of self-sustaining native fish, but in many, maybe even most cases, that's just not true. It's surprising how much mountain water is barren of fish for all practical purposes and how many of the populations of fish are the result of human intervention.

Before the arrival of what we sometimes grandly refer to as "civilization," many of the mountain streams and lakes were completely devoid of fish. In some of the highest lakes, no fish may have been there to begin with, either because there was no way for them to get there in the first place or because the habitat just wasn't fertile enough to support them. In other areas a natural disaster like a complete winterkill or the lake drying up for a few years wiped out whatever fish were there, and natural barriers downstream prevented repopulation.

The presence of fish in many of our mountain waters today is the result of some kind of artificial stocking program—though "program" isn't always the right word. Some of the early stocking efforts were primitive and haphazard by modern standards and actually contributed to the decline of native species by introducing fish with which the natives couldn't successfully compete. In other cases, inappropriate species were introduced (this usually translates into brook trout) that reproduced like rabiits, resulting in large populations of stunted fish.

Whatever part of the country you fish, natives—often called just that rather than brookies, cutthroats, or whatever—have a special romance about them, and there are still those of us who pine for the good old days. But the fact is that without the stockings—even the less-than-perfect ones—there would be a lot fewer fish than there are now, probably not enough to go around.

The Northern Colorado Rockies, where I do most of my high country fishing, are a good example. Once, only cutthroats were here, and most of them were in the major river systems with precious few in the remote high country. But now you can find brook trout, rainbows, rainbow/cutthroat crosses, some golden trout and grayling and even a few browns, as well as a few native cutts—some pure strain and some interbred. The native cutts still have that special magic, and I, along with a lot of other fishermen I know, sometimes go to great lengths to find and catch them. But I will happily fish for all the species present because they're good fish and because this state of affairs is, with a few notable exceptions, largely irreversible.

So how do you look at a map of a national park, state park, national forest, wilderness, or primitive area and figure out where the fish are? That's a good question with lots of answers.

Sooner or later, the streams flow out of the remote high country to cross a highway or enter a larger stream or river. These are the places where they're most often fished and where you can get your first handle on them.

An accessible mountain stream that yields, say, brook trout from under the highway bridge is usually worth wandering along for a mile or so, maybe even past the place where the inevitable fisherman's trail peters out, just to see what's up there. But you'd have to spend weeks to explore all the way up into the headwaters. All things considered, that wouldn't be a bad way to spend your time, but it is less than completely efficient.

A map, or a good *set* of maps, is the single most useful tool for the serious high country fisherman. Even a good map won't give you all the answers, but it will tell you whether you have a six- or eight-mile walk in front of you only to find that the stream gets smaller and smaller (and the fish, too) and finally ends in a series of trickles off a snowfield, or, ideally, that it leads you through meadows and beaver ponds to a headwater lake. If nothing else, a good map can save you a lot of fruitless trips, though not *all* fruitless trips.

Almost without exception, the topographic maps put out by the U.S. Geological Survey are the best ones you can get of any given area. They're accurate and show a surprising amout of detail. They are often available from local fly shops, sporting goods stores, outfitters, and mountaineering shops or from the U.S. Geological Survey, Denver, Colorado 80225 or Reston, Virginia 22092.

Local maps put out by specific national forests or state parks, county agencies (who can sometimes dig up aerial photos), and so on usually aren't as detailed as the U.S.G.S. maps, but they can sometimes provide additional clues and may also show you which areas are privately owned—good information to have.

In some popular fishing areas you can get commercial maps that show access points, major pools, and that sort of thing. The quality of these varies wildly, but on most I've seen the areas in which you're interested—the remote spots where most fishermen don't go—are represented by a few out-of-scale blue lines and dots with little or no useful detail.

I suppose I should point out here that, although I've used a lot of maps, the most useful ones were hand-drawn on the backs of bar napkins.

A good map will tell you what's up ahead, how steep the

climb is, and the location of major trails and landmarks. It will not, however, tell you where or how big the fish are, so let's apply a little logic to a hypothetical situation.

A decent-sized creek flows under a mountain highway or county road. Within earshot of the traffic, you've caught some six- to eight-inch brookies, and, just to make things tantalizing, a few small cutts. Now it's not unusual for the brook trout fishing to be better down by the road than it is farther upstream because the creek may be a little bigger and because the more or less steady fishing pressure will help keep the numbers down and the size of the fish up. On the other hand, a piece of dandy habitat upstream could hold some good fish, and those few cutthroats might also mean something.

So let's say that according to your map, the stream comes out of a fairly steep canyon that could well be little-fish water but above that, maybe a mile or two from the road, the lines on the topo map widen out, indicating a narrow meadow about a half mile long. The map shows no natural barrier, like a waterfall, between you and the meadow, so it's fair to assume that fish are there. They may be the same size as the ones you've already caught—and they may be smaller—but considering that a meadow stretch often provides better habitat than pocket water, the fish may also be a little bigger. Based on no more information than that, and since it isn't far, it's probably worth walking up there to have a look.

By the way, check the map for dirt roads. You may be able to drive up there in five minutes, although even if that's possible, you might still want to make the walk. The map won't show you those secret plunge pools where a big cutthroat may be hiding.

It's important to know where the passable dirt roads are and where they go for at least two reasons. Assuming you have a vehicle that will stand some rough use, a dirt road can save you a lot of walking. On the other hand, it will also do the same for a lot of other fishermen, and that nice, secluded-looking spot on the may may be heavily fished.

Check the course of the road as it relates to the course of

the stream carefully. If the two wander away from each other for a mile or so and the stream looks good (on the map) in that section, you may be looking at a spot that seldom gets fished. The absence of a trail is also a good sign.

I've checked out a number of places like that, especially when that lonely stretch of stream holds beaver ponds or what looks like a little meadow section, and the effort has been worthwhile a significant percentage of the time. This usually involves leaving the vehicle somewhere and bushwhacking cross-country to the water, and I have also discovered a new application of Murphy's Law. You remember Murphy's Law, "whatever can go wrong will." It applies to fishing on a startlingly regular basis.

What usually happens is this: you find the stream—it's, say, straight southwest and you follow a compass heading. On the way out you reverse the heading and, sure enough, find the road again. The problem is, you never, and I mean never, arrive right back at the car, and since those backcountry roads all look alike, you're never quite sure which way to go to find your car unless you're lucky enough to stumble on a very striking landmark that you remember passing on the way in. The application of Murphy's Law is that you will *always* walk down the road in the wrong direction.

I've tried to stack the deck by walking off in one direction for a hundred yards, then quickly turning around and going the other way, but it's never worked. Murphy's Law is like the law of gravity; there are no exceptions. The best advice I can give here is, don't tell anyone when you plan to be back—just say "I don't know, maybe late."

Another thing that a map won't tell you accurately is what kind of shape a four-wheel drive road is in. I've been on a few bad ones over the years and have even wounded a few vehicles badly enough to give them lots of character and seriously lower their resale value.

One of the worst I've ever been on (and have never been back to) was obviously designed to kill automobiles. I won't try to describe its entire bone-jarring length, but there is one spot where you drive along a stream—I mean *in* the stream— for about a quarter of a mile, then climb a steep hill and drop down an even steeper hill on the other side, at the bottom of which the road gets very narrow as it twists through a stand of spruce. The trouble is, of course, the drive up the stream has gotten your brakes wet, and, if you're not thinking about it, you come down that hill at about fifty miles per hour and rattle through the trees like the marble in a pinball machine. The ground in that stand of trees is littered with hubcaps, mirrors, door handles, broken glass, and other assorted parts, and it looks like the place where old jeeps go to die.

The point I'm trying to make here is that the symbol for the "road" on a map often involves some poetic license.

So let's say you've gotten to the meadow (one way or another) you saw on the map, and sure enough, it's a pretty spot with some deep runs and you've taken a few nice fish. Maybe there are even a few more cutthroats and one or two fish that are healthy and heavy. You find a comfortable log to sit on and have a sandwich, and you pass the time looking at the map, which tells you that a mile or so upstream is a gently sloping little valley dotted with beaver ponds.

At the bottom of the map it says the map was shot in the 1950s and was last field-checked in 1962. Beaver ponds come and go, and there's no way of telling what shape they were in even when the map was new, so by now there may not be much left. On the other hand, there may be some new ponds with nice brookies or maybe some good cutthroats. Again, there's no natural barrier and it's still early in the day, so you stroll up to have a look.

For the sake of argument, let's say at least some of the ponds are in good shape and you find some acceptable trout. Maybe you even fish the ponds carefully and take a fourteen incher, as well as some smaller fish. You're beginning to think you're onto something: the fish aren't huge, but there are plenty of them and they're wild and eager, and there's also little or no sign of other anglers—no clear trails, old bean cans, or fire pits.

Maps are tempting things, and the one you're looking at now tells you that on up above your beaver ponds is a pretty-looking lake hanging up near timberline. For that matter, there may be two or three, and the map also shows a waterfall or some very steep rapids (it's not always obvious which) between here and there.

An effective natural barrier tells you one thing: fish can't travel upstream from that point. In some cases, the water above a natural barrier—especially when that barrier occurs high up on a drainage—will be devoid of fish. In other cases, there will be the same kind of fish above and below, and in still others, a waterfall may separate the brook trout fishery from the higher waters that hold cutthroats, grayling, goldens, or whatever.

I know of a pretty little creek in the Rockies that holds all the six-inch brook trout you'd ever want to see. Some miles up it, however, is a spectacular waterfall, and above that is a large beaver pond. The pond holds grayling and cutthroats, the largest of which are in the fifteen- to sixteen-inch class. Above that is an alpine lake with grayling and goldens.

You'd never know about that just from looking at the map, but there are ways of finding out about such things, and so, sitting on your log at the head of the meadow, you decide not to make the rugged hike up to the lake on a wild guess. You shoulder your day pack and head back to do some research.

The most obvious way to find out about a piece of high country water is to ask the fishermen you know, or maybe the guy down at the local tackle shop: "ever fish so-and-so lake up above such-and-such?" That, of course, is often only a starting point. If the lake is, in fact, a good one, there will be times—rare times—when some good-hearted soul will tell you about it. But if you find someone who's fished it, and he tells you it's "full of little brookies," he may be telling the truth or he may be protecting a hell of a fine spot.

I've used the little brookie line myself a few times, and it works because it's so believable. A few years ago I was standing at the head of a big beaver pond catching pan-sized grayling with some regularity, and now and then a nice, fat cutthroat, when I spotted another fisherman coming up the trail. I tried to act like I didn't see him, but he stopped and watched me for a few minutes and then called out, "doing any good?" Out of the corner of my eye I saw the boil of a good-sized cutt, but I turned to him and said, as innocently as possible, "just a couple of little brookies."

The man thanked me and headed on up the trail. Amazing. I only wish I'd had a used car to sell. In other words, pay attention. I'm not the only liar out there. Also, it goes without saying that you'll get better information down at the fly shop if you've just bought a $600 cane fly rod—for cash—than if you just dropped in to chat and bum a free cup of coffee.

Evaluating rumors and advice is one of the greatest skills a fly fisherman can learn. Some information is good, some is bad (intentionally or otherwise), and a lot of it is just uninformed. There are a lot of fishermen who don't know how long twelve inches is and can't tell the difference between a rainbow and a cutthroat or a grayling and a whitefish. You have to consider the source, and secondhand information (some guy I met in a bar *told* me it was full of little brookies) is all but useless.

There are also inaccuracies on the other side. If someone whose judgment you don't have reason to trust tells you he caught twenty fifteen-inch cutthroats, subtract five inches from each fish and ten from the total number. The best information, of course, is firsthand from a close friend.

When you start asking around about a specific lake or stream, it's not uncommon to get no information at all or a lot of conflicting reports. If someone seems a bit *too* eager to tell you it's no good or gets a little panicky when the name of the place comes up, that's a good sign. Still, I'd hate to set out on a fifteen-mile overnighter based on nothing more than the look in someone's eyes. That look might be enough to make you want to check further, however.

On the other hand, someone who has a vested interest in having you believe the lake is just plain dynamite (like a guide who'd be more than happy to haul you up there for a price) may just be exaggerating things a bit.

With a few notable exceptions, most high country waters have been fished from time to time, though some very little, and they've also been surveyed by field biologists and/or stocked at some point. If anyone official has had anything to do with a piece of trout water, some sort of record exists. Ferreting out this kind of information can take time and effort, but if you're persistent, you can usually find someone who can tell you what you need to know.

Step one is to get in touch with the main office of whatever agency is in charge of the area in question, which will probably start you on your way through a string of referrals. If you ask about a couple of lakes and some beaver ponds in a state park (it's better to check out an area than just a single lake), you may get sent to the State Division of Wildlife, which may, in turn, send you to U.S. Fish and Wildlife or a professor of fisheries biology at the local university. Like I said, this can require some persistence. Keep in mind that you'll get more cooperation if you're patient and courteous and are willing to sit through long explanations of things you don't really care about when the occasion arises. I've been pleasantly surprised at how helpful most of the people I've dealt with in this way have been. Of course, as time goes by, you'll learn who and who not to call.

I've known some people to go to great lengths to get good information on remote trout waters. A good friend of mine, Paul, just recently volunteered to do some kind of survey work up in one of the national parks. This involved an overnight camp-out and some grunt labor, but the head research biologist happened to be along on the trip. In the evening after the work was done, Paul, with the help of a bottle of good whiskey, managed to wangle some very interesting and little known facts about some of the more obscure area waters. While it's still fresh, I'll have to invest my own bottle to get some of that out of Paul.

There will, of course, be those rare times when you'll get

in touch with the field biologist who just finished an in-depth study of the lake in question. He'll tell you how many fish there are, what kind, how big, whether or not they're a self-sustaining population, what kind of insects are present in what numbers and/or percentages, and a whole lot of other information that you probably won't care about or, if you're like me, won't be able to understand.

In most cases, however, you won't be that lucky. You'll get marginal information like "our records show that it was stocked with cutthroats (or whatever) in 1969" or "our most recent records show that brook trout are there." Sometimes you'll be told that, for one reason or another, the lake is barren of fish, which is also useful information.

If all you can find out about a lake is that it holds a breeding population of fish, it's probably worth a try. Reproducing populations of brookies often mean stunted fish, but that's not always the case. Especially if there are several lakes, a stream, and some ponds, it's not unusual for a few good fish to be lurking around somewhere. If the area holds goldens, grayling, or cutthroats, go for it.

If the lake in question does not allow for spawning (one question that you should always ask your source), it's important to know if it was stocked, when, and with what size and kind of fish. A lake that does not allow for reproduction and that was stocked four or five years ago with fry (and that, as far as your source knows, hasn't winterkilled lately) stands a good chance of holding some very large trout. The ideal spot is a remote lake with, at best, marginal possibilities for spawning that was stocked with cutthroat or golden fry about five years ago and that is lousy with freshwater shrimp. The absence of a trail would also be a nice touch. This is all information that you can learn with nothing more than a map and a telephone.

If you run into a dead end with all the local, state, and federal agencies, try looking up any private groups, like fish and game clubs, who might have done some stocking.

In some cases, you don't even have to do a lot of detective work—all you have to do is keep abreast of the local news and speculation. Some of the best brook trout fishing I've had in recent years came about through the greenback cutthroat trout recovery program in Rocky Mountain National Park. The greenback recovery team had poisoned out a series of beaver ponds and restocked them with the once-thought-to-be-extinct greenbacks. The cutts did well, but somewhere along the line, a few brookies got back in and, being aggressive feeders, they started to get nice and big. When the ponds were finally opened to fishing, anglers were required to release the greenbacks and encouraged to keep the brookies.

Many fishermen did, in fact, eat the brook trout, but some of us put them back and, as their numbers dwindled, their size increased. There aren't many left now, but many of them are quite large, and the U.S. Fish and Wildlife officials are begging fishermen to take them out because they're out-competing the cutthroats. If Bruce Rosenlund, head of the project, is reading this—Bruce, I apologize, but I just can't bring myself to kill a fourteen-inch high country beaver pond brookie with a hooked jaw like a salmon and a shape like a late season summer squash—force of habit.

I've been talking a lot about lakes here because lakes are what you can get the best information on. In most cases, you'll be able to learn little or nothing about the streams and ponds in the area from official sources. However, if the stream lower down holds fish and so do the headwater lakes, you can bet that there are fish in between. In some areas the stream and the ponds are actually better than the lakes themselves and are definitely worth checking out. In fact, rumor has it that more than one western state record fish that was supposed to have come from this or that lake came, in fact, from a nearby beaver pond instead. If you're looking at an area for an extended trip, it's a good idea to pick a spot with lots of water—maybe two or three lakes and a nice string of beaver ponds.

It's amazing how different one lake can be from the next, or one pond from another for that matter, even if they're only a stone's throw apart.

Working your way far into the backcountry to catch fish from a lake or stream that no one knows much about is a truly excellent experience, but you don't always have to mount a major expedition to score well. It's sad but fortunate that most fishermen are easily pleased; that is, if there's a stocked lake they can drive right to and set up a lawn chair, then that's where they fish. Such spots serve a number of useful purposes, not the least of which is to divert attention from nearby waters— sometimes only a few hundred yards from the road—that can be quite good and very lightly fished.

I can think of several spots like that just in the mountains near my home: areas where the second lake—in the trees a few hundred yards up the slope—provides good fishing simply because the one down by the road takes all the pressure. Spots like this all seem to have one thing in common: the existence of the second lake, beaver pond, or whatever is not obvious to the casual observer but is a clear, though often small, blue spot on the local map.

Of course, if there's a wide trail to the second lake and its shore is littered with old bait cans and snelled hook packages, you probably haven't found the secret, hidden spot. If the place seems to be relatively unknown, however, it's worth looking into, but there is one basic rule that must be followed: *don't let people see you going up there.*

I like to shoulder my way through the crowd of bait fishers and make a good show of heading off in the wrong direction. Once I'm back in the trees and out of sight, I can swing around and go where I'm going. My friend Mike Clark likes to make an equally big show of getting a roll of toilet paper out of the back pocket of his vest and heading for the bushes. When there's a big enough crowd around, no one seems to notice that he never comes out.

It's almost always worth taking a look at the streams, beaver ponds, and second or third lakes within a mile or so of heavily fished, easily accessible high country waters, especially if the lake by the road is stocked regularly with "catchable"-sized trout. The stockers will put a lot of fishermen off the place and will keep a lot of others sitting happily within earshot of their car radios. The same is true of lakes and ponds a little way off of clearly marked trails. The majority of fishermen seem to just "go to the lake" without looking around very much.

So far these are all things you can work out for yourself, using not much more than your feet and your native intelligence, but I should say a few words about guides. I do most of my prospecting in areas that I know fairly well (always an advantage) and have a small network of close friends who do the same. I'm also not what you'd call a wealthy sportsman type. In fact, I've been the guide more often than I've been the client. Still, I have been guided a few times in unfamiliar territory, and can testify to the truth of the old saying: "there's nothing better than a good guide and nothing worse than a bad one."

A good guide is one who knows the area well and who will work with you to put together the kind of trip you want to take. He won't fish all day himself—the best ones won't fish at all unless you invite them to—he'll offer help and suggestions only when they're appropriate, and he won't try to land your fish for you.

The best way to locate a good guide is through one or more of his former sports, preferably ones you know and trust. In any case, do as much checking as possible beforehand. The cost? It will vary greatly, but a good guide is worth his weight in gold, and a bad one should pay *you* for dragging him along.

There are a lot of ways to go about taking a guided trip, and each has its advantages if things go well. Styles range all the way from one of the local boys showing you a good lake for a few dollars to a full-blown expedition where the "staff" packs in the gear, sets up camp, ties your fly on for you, leads you by the hand to the right casting spot, does the cooking, washes the dishes, and wakes you the next morning with a fresh cup of coffee. At least that's what I hear.

Naturally, you get what you pay for, and one of the most economical and efficient ways to go is the spot pack, where a wrangler with a horse or two packs your party's gear in for you and leaves you at the lake. You can walk along or ride a horse of your own for a little extra change. After a few days of fishing, you simply walk out, which isn't much of a problem because you've eaten up all the provisions, making the load lighter by 75 percent, and the trip out is almost always downhill. In some cases, you can arrange for the guide to come back and pick you up at a pre-determined time.

There is one very important rule about hiring a guide, and that is, *let yourself be guided*. Theoretically, you're paying for expert advice. If you think you know more about it than the guide does, why hire him in the first place? If he tells you to bring a heavy rod, chest waders, and certain fly patterns, do it. Do a little research beforehand, then have a little faith.

Most good high country fishing spots are the result of some combination of research, rumor, and exploration. I admit that I've been led to, or carefully directed to, many of the good waters I now know of, but I've also found a few myself, and those have been the best in terms of personal satisfaction. I have, naturally, been pretty closemouthed about these places, only partly for selfish reasons.

My friend Archie (A.K.) Best has a formula for these things: everyone you tell about a fishing spot will tell at least two other people, who will, in turn, tell two other people, and so on. I think that's what they call a geometric progression. Whatever you call it, it's never good. Being able to remember when the fishing was better might qualify you as an old-timer, but it's not a pleasant feeling.

You will want to let your friends in on the good places you know of, but try doing it this way: don't *tell them* about a lake or stream, *take them there*. Once they've seen it, fished it, and learned how good it is, they'll start thinking of it as *their* secret spot, not just someplace they heard was good. For the benefit of strangers, friends of friends, and people met in bars, all you caught was "a bunch of little brookies," and if you must brag about your fish, disguise the location.

A little chop on the water and some cloud cover—a perfect day.

Weather, Seasons, and Cycles

THE CONCEPT OF HITTING THE water "right"—at the right time of year, on the right day, at the right *time* of day—is central to fly-fishing, and it's one of the more important elements of fishing in the high mountains. Being on the water at that cosmic moment when the fishing is at its best is a hard enough thing to schedule on the famous lowland rivers, where you can check a hatch chart or call the local fly shop and ask if the Green Drakes are on yet. On a mountain lake or a string of beaver ponds, that kind of intelligence usually doesn't exist for two reasons: it's probably not fished enough for that kind of information to have been compiled (which is one of the reasons why you're going there), and chances are conditions change so much on a daily to yearly basis that events of interest to fly fishermen don't happen on anything like a regular schedule. For instance, there's a mountain lake not far from here that's well known for its speckled dun hatch, but it is also well known that, although the hatch only seems to last for a week or so, it can begin at any time within about a ten-week period. I've managed to hit it twice in five years, only because other people have stumbled on it and told me about it.

Another problem is that the seasons are all out of proportion. At the highest fishable altitudes, spring, summer,

and fall can pass in ten or twelve weeks, even less in a bad
season, and the rest of the year—forty or forty-two weeks of
it—is, for all practical purposes, the off-season. It's always
amazed me that trout and grayling can even survive under
those conditions, let alone grow to good size, but in the right
kind of water, they can do it.

Of course, it's not all that rugged. The fishing season lasts
longer at the lower altitudes, and in some of the areas that
one calls the foothills and another calls mountains, it can be
nearly as long as it is out on the flatlands. Moving uphill in
the mountains is like moving north on the globe. In the real
high country what passes for summer puts in only a brief
appearance the way it does, say, up around the arctic circle.
There will also be those years when winter stays late and
returns early.

But altitude and the severity of the weather aren't the only
variables. A lake or pond that lies in the shade of a deep
canyon, for instance, will probably stay frozen longer than
one at the same altitude that lies out in an open meadow,
and snow and ice will stay longer on a north-facing slope
than on a south-facing one.

A "day" will also be shorter on a piece of water that lies
in the shade of a mountain slope on one side or the walls of
a canyon on both sides. Midday remains about the same, but
morning and evening can take on new meanings, and it's
not unusual for trout in a high lake to wait until the sun hits
the water to start feeding and stop the minute it's off, though
that's certainly not always the case.

It might seem logical that a lake with a long growing season
would grow bigger fish than a lake with a short one, but
that's apparently not true. The amount of food available to
the fish on a regular basis seems to be what determines the
growth rate. That's why you can find little fish in a foothill
lake and big fish in a pond at 11,000 feet.

If you're curious as to whether a certain lake is open early
in the year (early meaning something like late June), it
sometimes works to find another lake at about the same
altitude that's right by a road. Check that one before you

hike up to the one that really interests you. Also, try and find a control lake that's in the same kind of terrain. If you're lucky, you might be able to locate a park ranger or local private pilot who has flown over the area recently who can tell you what is and what isn't open.

Getting into a high lake in the first week or two after the ice has gone off can be a ticklish affair involving some guesswork and maybe even a pair of snowshoes, but it can be worth the trouble. The fish wake up hungry after the long winter, and they often feed ravenously. The fishing can be fast and furious, though the fish are sometimes a little thin. It's always worth trying to hit a lake that you know to hold good fish right at ice-out.

Some friends and I hit a good cutthroat lake this last spring just about two or three weeks after ice-out. We had some excellent fishing, although we had to wait for it. Things didn't really start to happen until late afternoon, and we guessed that maybe the sun had to warm the water a little first. It was cold as a glass of iced tea, and for the same reason. There were still a few chunks of ice floating in it.

The high country fishing season in most areas runs roughly from late June through late August or early September with, naturally, variations due to altitude, latitude, and the yearly weather patterns. Midsummer is what we're talking about. The higher up in the mountains you go, the more the season shrinks on either end, and way up above timberline you're often looking at the four or five weeks that comprise late July and early August as prime fishing season.

The spring runoff that muddies the lower rivers also happens in the high country streams, but it's less severe and often of shorter duration, starting later and ending earlier. In June, when the lower rivers are high and muddy, you can often find some clear water up in the feeder creeks and be taking trout on dry flies while most fishermen are down at the local fly shop crying about how lousy the fishing is.

The water in the high streams will be cold that early, sometimes too cold for much fish or bug activity, so the best thing to do is to look for the lowest altitude streams that are still clear and work up into the tributaries. These early periods are often quite short—a matter of weeks—and more than once I've seen the weather turn warm and all the high creeks muddy at the same time. Still, it's worth looking into. By the time the high streams start to run off, some of the lower lakes and ponds will be open.

Midsummer is the best time to fish the high mountains, and it's also the most comfortable. Mid-morning and early evening rises are common, and midday fishing, especially in the streams and ponds, can also be productive. There will be slow periods and perhaps some tough fishing, but high country trout, except for those in the richest of waters, seldom get as lazy and self-satisfied as their lowland cousins. They'll be on the lookout for food under all but the worst conditions. These fish have to attain a year's growth in a short time, and they just can't afford to be too picky.

Autumn is one of the best times to fish for trout anywhere, and it comes early in the high country. The fish are as fat as they'll get, and they'll be eager to fatten up some more for the long winter ahead. "Autumn" may come as early as the last part of August, and it can be easy to miss, though in an easygoing year, high country fishing can be good, if spotty, well into September.

If you were going to spend a whole season fishing the mountains, you'd want to start lower down in June, work your way up to hit the high alpine lakes through midsummer, then ease back down the slope as late August and September approached—about the way the elk herds move and at about the same pace.

The weather in the mountains can be mild for days on end, or it can be wild and changeable. It's seldom accurately reflected in the local weather reports, except after the fact. Phrases like "possible showers and wind in the high country" are of little use—showers and wind are *always* possible. One thing the weather report will tell you, however, is how much colder it gets in the high country than it does down on the flats, especially at night. Always carry rain gear and some warm clothing, even on a day trip.

All things considered, a cloudy day is better than a bright sunny one.

Predictable or not, we tend to think of the weather in terms of our own personal comfort, but as every flyfisher knows, it can profoundly affect the fishing as well. Most of the old saws about weather and fishing apply well to the high country: all things being equal, a cloudy day is better than a bright, sunny one because the fish seem more confident about rising to the surface or moving into the shallows to feed. It's also been said that the wings of freshly hatched midges and mayflies take longer to dry on a cloudy day, keeping the bugs on the water longer and making a rise to dry flies more likely.

A cloudy day can even go so far as to kick up a little wind, a light drizzle, or even a little snow, and the fishing will still be good. In fact, conditions like that are often the best. I think a hard rain will put fish off of feeding on or near the surface, but I'll admit that I haven't fished in enough hard rains to test that sufficiently. A heavy rain seldom lasts long in the high country, and I usually retreat to the bank and the shelter of a poncho to wait it out, though I'm often haunted by the words of my Uncle Leonard: "the fish don't care if it rains, they're already wet." After a rain the fishing will often get quite good for a while as the fish rise to the bugs that were washed in.

My personal rule here is that I'll fish in a *drizzle* but not in a *rain* , but I can't give you a strict definition of those terms. I guess if I'm catching trout, it's drizzling, and if I'm not, it's raining. One thing to remember is that getting wet and cold can spell trouble. It's a lot easier to *stay* dry than to get that way once you're soaked.

Anything from a gentle breeze to a stiff wind can also be good, although the latter can make casting a real chore, and I guess I'll go so far as to say that bad weather—wind, rain, clouds, drizzle, etc.—is consistently the best weather to fish in, at least on the lakes.

Of course, trout and grayling *do* feed in nice weather, and they're far from uncatchable, but you'll often be looking at longer, finer leaders, maybe smaller flies, and a lot more stealth. If the opportunity presents itself, I'll often go find a little stretch of pocket water to fish when it's bright and calm and come back to the lake or the beaver pond when the storm starts rolling in.

Speaking of storms rolling in: a friend of mine claims that trout can sense the difference in pressure when a front moves into the area and that this will make them feed more actively. I can't imagine why that would be true, but he and I have acted on it a few times and done very well by hitting a good piece of water just as a big low pressure system came in. We've also gotten rained, hailed, and snowed on a few times.

What the weather does can make a big difference in the fishing. *When* it does it can be just as important. A cloud bank and a cool breeze moving in in the late morning to mid-afternoon can make the fish more active and bring up the larger trout, and the aftermath of a rain squall before, say, 4:00 in the afternoon can trigger a nice rise. Any of those things happening along toward evening can put the fish down early, and in the morning they can postpone things.

In the summer, the trout and grayling in the high country are likely to be active throughout the daylight hours, with the inevitable slow periods. In most cases, mornings and evenings are best with the slowest periods coming near the middle of the day. That's assuming daylong fair weather. Changes in the weather will often supercede time of day by the clock. In the spring and fall, the best times usually occur during the middle and toward the end of the day, when it's warmest.

In my experience and that of other anglers I've talked with, trout and grayling in the high coutry waters don't feed at night. That may be a disappointment to head hunters who are used to taking their biggest fish at night, but it also means the big fish will feed during the day when you can see what you're doing—a fair trade, I think. Keep in mind, though, that the bigger fish will still prefer low light conditions.

There are also population cycles to deal with in the high country that can affect the size and numbers of fish in a given piece of water from season to season. A new beaver pond on an otherwise marginal brook trout stream may well have good-sized fish in it for a few seasons before the first residents die off and their offspring overpopulate the place. If something like that happens near home, it's worth repeated trips just to watch the process. A lake with no spawning areas that has been stocked with rainbow or cutthroat fry may well grow a single generation of big fish that will be there for a few seasons before they vanish. A decent lake that's been winterkilled may appear devoid of fish the following spring, but a few years later, the survivors may have grown nice and large because of the reduced competition for food.

Also, keep track of any programs seeking to reestablish native strains of trout. Many waters that come under these programs will stay closed for years as the fish establish themselves and will then be opened quietly with little or no publicity. Another good bet is any new state lease on formerly private water. Almost any water that has been fished very lightly, or not at all, for a good long time is worth a try.

Some of these things are difficult to research from a distance. In fact, they're sometimes hard to see when they're going on right under your nose, and often what happened only becomes evident in hindsight. Still, they can be producers of good fishing and big fish—sometimes on only a temporary basis—and they're worth watching.

A piece of water with a stable reproducing population of big trout is, of course, the ideal, and these conditions still exist in the high country, though they get a little harder to come by every season. It's the cycles, however, that will leave fishermen standing on the banks of a high lake scratching their heads and saying, "I can't understand it. Two years ago this was full of big cutts."

A.K. on the Frying Pan River.

The Frying Pan

I'VE DONE A LOT OF THE WORK on the final draft of this book here on the Frying Pan River in Colorado in a cabin owned by Bill Fitzsimmons. It's the last of September, and Archie (A.K.) Best and I are here fishing the Blue-winged Olive hatch—not the Green Drake hatch we'd planned on, but no complaints.

I don't usually like working on vacations—either the work or the play suffers, if not both—but it was either this or not fish the Frying Pan in September, which was unthinkable. In fact, it's worked out well, since A.K., who's a professional fly tier, also had some chores to do. I should take this opportunity to thank him for tying me a half dozen quill bodied #18 mayflies last night while I pecked away at the typewriter.

At first it seemed a little incongruous to be writing about high country backpack fly fishing while living in a cabin with a wood stove, refrigerator, and real beds, but then I remembered a quote about poetry. Somebody (Wordsworth? Pope?) said that poetry consisted of strong emotions reflected upon in tranquility, and that's sort of what this has been— remote camps reflected upon around a kitchen table.

We've had some slow days and some fast ones on the river, and we've both caught a fair number of trout, though

I honestly can't say how many. We've only taped two fish so far—mine was seventeen and one-quarter inches and A.K.'s was a little over eighteen (we measured them because we figured they were both twenty). It doesn't matter, though, because by this time next year they'll both be "about twenty" anyway.

My fish, by the way, was a complete surprise. The rise looked small, and he came from about the last place in that stretch that I'd have expected to hook a big trout. So it goes.

I've always liked fishing with A.K. because we think alike and because we only measure our fishing success in terms of numbers or size of trout on those days when we're catching big ones or a lot of them. We both tend to quickly lose track of the number of fish we've caught, and that makes for a pleasant absence of competition.

That's when things are going well. At other times—the majority of times, I suppose,—we're usually content just to have fish to work over and problems to solve. A.K. is one of those guys who can spend hours working over a single fish, either because it's a big one or simply because he's fascinated with the problem. I have less patience than that, but I'm learning. There is, for instance, a big rainbow sitting down there right now with one of my flies in his jaw. He took it after about two hours of casting and waiting and changing flies, and the fact that I couldn't land him doesn't bother me as much as it once would have. He was big, he was feeding in a hard spot, and I fooled him,—that's the point. And anyway, a mystery unsolved (like is he really as big as I think he is?) is more tantalizing.

Generally on a long stay like this, A.K. and I have all the problems of humankind solved in the first three days, and we're right on schedule this time. If the world were run by people like us, it would be a much better and simpler place. Now the talk (with the occasional philosophical footnote) is all about fishing. How is it, for instance, that the long tails of a mayfly spinner are contained in the shorter tails of the dun, which are, in turn, contained in the still shorter tails of the nymph? Are they coiled up in there or what? And why?

We've also observed that life is like a trout stream in that both start roughly at point A and end up more or less at point B, but that it's the journey that's worthwhile, not the destination. Sure it's corny—also true.

So fly-fishing is great and the trout aren't all of it—maybe not even the largest part of it when all is said and done—I imagine we're all more or less in agreement on that.

Unfortunately, trout fishing isn't what it once was. In a few ways it may be better; in most ways it's worse. We can blame some of it on irrigation, diversion, pollution, development, and all the other blessings of civilization, and we can do what we can about those things as our own politics, consciences, and inclinations dictate.

I don't mean to toss that off, either. A lot can be done—some of it already *has* been done—to slow, stop, or even reverse the destruction of trout waters and general wildlife habitat by people who have done everything from running for office to spending the price of a movie and dinner once a year to join a conservation group.

One thing we can all do, however, is not contribute to the destruction ourselves. I met a man once who told me he and some friends had "fished out" a high country lake. They brought out something like twenty pounds of cutthroat fillets, and he told me proudly that the going was so rough they had to "dynamite some beaver ponds just to get the vehicles through." That's my worst horror story to date that doesn't involve a government agency.

Most of us don't do things like that, and the few of us who do are beyond help, but there are a lot of lesser offenses, and they add up. How many times have you hiked in several miles to a lake only to find empty bean cans, beer bottles, and wads of cellophane lying around? I don't know who's responsible for that—no one I know. Most of the people who I fish with or run into on the water not only carefully stow their own garbage, but they usually pack out the stuff that others have left. It takes five minutes, and I've never seen anyone stagger under the extra weight.

Even if someone has no common sense, there are rules

posted, and you can't go too far wrong if you obey them. "No littering" is one that is—or should be—at the top of every list. "No pets" or "all pets on leashes" is another. This, of course, means dogs, and it's a good rule. Now don't get me wrong, I love dogs—I've had one all my life—but I don't take them into the backcountry loose where they can chase down fawns and calf elk (and they will, too, no matter how cute and cuddly they are at home).

A sign that says "no motorized vehicles beyond this point" should be obeyed upon pain of death. I've seen a few of those signs that add "... because of habitat damage," and one could also add "... because of damage to human sensibilities, not to mention the relative peace of the local wildlife." Once again, don't get me wrong. I'm a four-wheeler from way back, but I keep it on the roads, some of which are plenty tough enough.

If the regulations say "no camping without permit" or "no fires," then get a permit and don't build a fire. You can use one of those portable camp stoves—they're cheap, light, convenient, and are, in fact, much more efficient for cooking than a wood fire.

Things like that sometimes seem arbitrary and ridiculous, but the permit system is usually a way to avoid having hordes of people in a given area at any one time (better for you if you *are* there), and a no-fires rule makes sense if someone tells you it's because all the campfires in the area are using up the dead wood and keeping the nutrients from returning to the soil. If you insist on building fires in a no-fires area, you may be part of the reason why the place will look like the dark side of the moon in another fifty years. Or maybe it's just a temporary thing. Maybe it's been a dry year and the fire danger is unusually high.

I'm like you,—I like to know the reason for things. I've found that if you call up the appropriate agency, someone there will be happy to explain things.

Among the biggest dangers are people like me who have been out in the woods for a long time and who consider themselves to be pretty competent outdoorsmen. It's tempting for us to believe that the rules are for the weekend city kids and not for us. Don't believe it for a second—everyone thinks that, and, in fact, its the best woodsmen I know who go to the greatest lengths to obey the rules.

What we're talking about is trying to leave things the way you found them, and that brings us to the fish themselves. I won't tell you to release every trout you catch (except, of course, in areas where you're required to do that by law), but I'll ask you to consider the possibility. Fisheries biologists will tell you that catch and release fishing isn't the grand, all-encompassing solution that some of us like to think it is, and I suppose they're right. In overpopulated brook trout waters, for instance, the fisherman who releases his trout is probably doing more harm than good. In some places the regulations reflect that by extending the bag limit on brook trout under eight inches.

There are other exceptions, too, but when you're fishing over wild, healthy fish of good size, I think it's fair to say you're doing the right thing by releasing most, if not all, of the ones you catch. When you've gone, the fish will still be there, both for you the next time you come and for the next fisherman who hikes up the trail and maybe—in a symbolic way, at least—for your children and grandchildren. At the very least, you'll have left them the way you found them.

To date, A.K. and I haven't killed any fish on this trip. We're doing most of our fishing up in the catch and release area, but that's not the reason. We could easily go downstream where it's legal to keep one brown and one rainbow, and we've been talking about doing that, just for a ceremonial trout dinner. Chances are we'll never get around to it, though, because we're just out of the habit, and anyway, A.K. and I have this thing for Dinty Moore canned beef stew.

Speaking of which, the cabin is filled with the aroma of stew at this moment, and A.K. just got up from his fly tying to stir it. One of Bill's cats is leering in through the window, attracted by the smell, and I'll bet a dollar that if I opened the door right now, his two Chesapeake Bay retrievers, Trapper and Tonkin, would be out there wagging their tails in unison, expecting a handout. It's cold tonight and the fire feels good. We're burning aspen and it's popping a lot—one of those fires that really wants to get out of the stove and onto the rug.

There will probably be a hard frost tonight, but probably only down here in the canyon with the river, and the hatch may start a little later tomorrow than it did today. That's because time is different in a place like this. Here things happen when they're damn well ready and not before. It's refreshing.

They say you forget your troubles on a trout stream, but that's not quite it. What happens is that you begin to see where your troubles fit into the grand scheme of things, and suddenly they're just not such a big deal anymore.

Near Basalt, Colorado
September 22, 1983

Index